MARKETING

·····································

A MULTIPLE-CHOICE
STUDY GUIDE

MARKETING

A MULTIPLE-CHOICE STUDY GUIDE

Everett M. Jacobs

PITMAN PUBLISHING

Dedicated to my wife Barbara
'Fraig mir nisht kayn shaylas'

PITMAN PUBLISHING
128 Long Acre, London WC2E 9AN

A Division of Pearson Professional Limited

First published in Great Britain in 1995

© Everett M. Jacobs, 1995

ISBN 0 273 60280 2

British Library Cataloguing in Publication Data
A CIP catalogue record for this book can be obtained from the British Library

1   3   5   7   9   10   8   6   4   2

Typeset by 🐦 Tek Art, Croydon, Surrey
Printed and bound in Great Britain by Clays Ltd, St Ives plc

The Publishers' policy is to use paper manufactured from sustainable forests.

CONTENTS

PREFACE

WHY USE THIS BOOK?

This book has been written with three types of people and their different needs in mind: marketing students, general readers and practitioners interested in marketing, and marketing lecturers.

Marketing students will find its 1,000 questions, covering twenty major subject areas, useful in preparing for essay, as well as multiple-choice, examinations. By allowing them to test their competence across a wide range of marketing topics, the book should help them to improve both their understanding of marketing and their examination performance in three ways: by learning from the great variety of questions spanning the most important areas of contemporary marketing, by allowing them to pinpoint their specific strengths and weaknesses, and also by directing their attention to areas requiring further study. In presenting the questions in a multiple-choice format, the book should also help familiarize students with this increasingly popular style of examination and facilitate their checking of answers.

Many general readers and marketing practitioners outside the academic world are rightly interested in marketing as an important business discipline rather than as an examination topic. The book allows them to test their understanding and competence in marketing, and at the same time deepen their insight into marketing through the numerous case studies and examples.

Marketing lecturers will find the book a convenient classroom aid for reviewing and discussing major marketing topics and issues. The questions are far less stereotyped, more challenging, more varied in form, and hopefully, with the case studies and examples, more interesting than those typically found in the lecturer's guide to a text book. A wide range of popular marketing texts and related books has been used in the preparation of the questions, making the book suitable for most courses.

To maximize the usefulness of the book for teaching purposes, the answer to every fifth question has been withheld. The Instructor's Manual (available to lecturers adopting this book) contains the answers to these questions, and explanations to all questions. For lecturers contemplating setting their own multiple-choice examinations, tests, or quizzes, the Instructor's Manual also contains a discussion of multiple-choice examinations, a methodology for setting multiple-choice questions, and an explanation of computer-marking of multiple-choice examinations.

FORMAT OF THE BOOK

The book consists of twenty sections, each containing fifty questions, which cover the main subject areas of marketing. The answer to every fifth question has been withheld to enable the book to be used for classroom review and discussion. The answers to all other questions appear at the end of the book.

The questions have been chosen to cover a wide range within each subject area. It should be stressed that the object is to find out how much you know, not to try to show how little you know. There are no trick questions.

For each question, the single correct answer is A, B, C, D, or E. In some questions designed to test reasoning and evaluation more closely, it is indicated that two alternatives (from statements 1, 2, 3, 4, and 5), taken together, make up the correct answer (A, B, C, D, or E). In some of these questions, it is possible that as many as three alternatives (say 1, 4, and 5) are acceptable, but in that event, only one combination of two alternatives is correct. In this example, the correct answer would be E (grouping together statements 4 and 5), since no answer groups together either 1 and 4 or 1 and 5. The sequence of answers has been chosen absolutely at random.

The questions have been pre-tested, and range in facility from relatively easy (with the expectation that up to 80 per cent will answer correctly) to difficult (with the expectation that only 25 to 30 per cent will answer correctly). In terms of discrimination (the difference between the proportion of the top quartile of candidates getting the question right and the proportion of the bottom quartile of candidates getting the question right), the range is from about 20 to 60 per cent. A balance between easier and more difficult questions has been built into each section. More difficult questions, judged in terms of facility and discrimination, are indicated by an asterisk (*) next to the question number.

The questions test both theory and practice, and so far as possible avoid definitions. Some questions test the so-called 'lower level' skills of knowledge and comprehension, but wherever possible, an effort has been made to test the so-called 'higher level' skills of application, analysis, synthesis, and evaluation. Of course, it is impossible to test the higher level skill of expression in a multiple-choice framework, but with that exception, the skills we should most look for in essays are assessed in this book. The ability of multiple-choice examinations to do this, while at the same time allowing us to use computers for marking, is one of the great labour-saving benefits available from this assessment method.

HOW TO USE THE BOOK

To get the most from the book, you should be familiar with the subject area before attempting the questions. The book is not intended to replace text books, lectures, or practical experience, although you should be able to increase your marketing competence and knowledge from mastering the material covered in the questions.

It is advisable to try to answer all the questions in a section before you look at the answers. If you are timing yourself, allow a maximum of ninety minutes for each section. Naturally, it is possible to look at the answers as you go along, but this is recommended only for those who habitually check solutions to crossword puzzle clues as they progress through the puzzle. Where answers have been withheld, you can look up the subject in a text, compare notes with a friend, or, in classroom situations, consult with the lecturer. Once you have completed the section and have checked the answers, you should be able to see your strengths and weaknesses. The results should guide you in your further study of marketing.

As a general measure of your competence in any given area, an unadjusted score of 40 or more correct is excellent; 30–39 good; 25–29 fair; 20–24 passing; and 19 or less, requires more work. Of course, in a multiple-choice examination, deductions may be made for incorrect answers, and you may be given the opportunity to not answer a question. These considerations may affect your final score under examination conditions. Therefore, a good strategy for dealing with multiple-choice examinations is advisable.

SUGGESTED STRATEGY FOR MULTIPLE-CHOICE EXAMINATIONS

Many multiple-choice examinations are composed of 100 questions to be answered in three hours. You build up your score by answering correctly as many questions as possible. To discourage guessing, some marking schemes deduct a fixed amount (usually 0.25 points) for each incorrect answer when there are five alternatives: pure guessing should result on average in 20 correct answers, which when divided by 80 incorrect answers, equals 0.25 points for each incorrect answer.

In order not to force you to guess when you are unsure of an answer, some marking schemes allow you to offer no answer to the question (sometimes expressed as the alternative '? - Not offering an answer'). If you choose this alternative, you will neither benefit nor be penalized for this question. However, if you choose '?' too often, you may reduce the number of answers to the level where you will not score enough points from correctly answered questions to get a good mark.

Assuming that guessing is penalized and you have the chance not to answer a question, the following strategy should benefit you.

- *When all else fails, read the examination instructions.* If you are told to make a solid bold mark, in pencil, in the appropriate box on a computer card, do just that. If you are told to circle your answer on an answer sheet, do so. If you are told not to, do not remove the examination paper from the examination room. You will make life easier for everyone, including yourself, if you follow the instructions.

- Unlike essay examinations, it is *not* a good idea to read through all 100 questions before answering any. This will take you too long.

- If the questions are grouped under subject headings, look at the headings and put into a priority order those you are most confident about. For the subject you have given first priority, answer all the questions you are confident about, and leave the rest. You can go back to them later. Then move on to your second priority, answer all the questions you can, and leave the rest. Do the same for your third through to last priority.

- If the questions are not grouped under subject headings, go through the paper question by question, and answer all the questions you are confident about. If you have difficulty with a given question, there is no need to worry. Leave it, and go to a question you *can* answer. Concentrate on finding questions you *can* answer before attempting questions you find more difficult.

- After you have gone through the paper answering the questions you can answer, there will be two types of questions left: those you are not quite sure about, and those where you are very unsure.

- Since it is in your interest to answer as many questions as possible, you should first try to answer those that you are not quite sure about. Blind guessing is penalized, so the best procedure is to eliminate at least two alternatives before answering. This will give you one chance in two, or one chance in three, of being right. At these odds, it is probably worth the risk to guess. If you are still uncertain and do not want to gamble, leave the question, go on to the next you are unsure about, and again try to eliminate at least two alternatives. Carry on until you have gone through all these questions.

For questions where you are very unsure, it is best not to guess, for reasons explained above. However, elimination of at least two alternatives for such a question may make it worth guessing, as explained.

- For all questions where you have decided not to offer an answer, indicate where appropriate that you are not answering the question (mark the '?' on your computer card, or circle that alternative on your answer sheet).

- Towards the end of the examination, before handing in your computer card or answer sheet, check to *make sure that you have answered all questions*, even if your answer to a question is '?' If you fail to submit an answer to a question, some computer programs mark it as if it were incorrect.

ACKNOWLEDGEMENTS

I would not have undertaken the long task of writing this book had it not been for the unbounded enthusiasm and faith of Ms Jennifer Mair, at the time a commissioning editor at Pitman Publishing. She heard a paper I gave on multiple-choice examinations for marketing at the Marketing Education Group's annual conference in Cardiff in 1991, and pretty much insisted both that I had to write this book (which I was not intending to do at the time), and that she had to have it for Pitman. She, and her successor, Mr Keith Stanley, provided me with much appreciated encouragement through the seemingly countless months of writing and question-testing.

I am also most grateful to present and past colleagues at the Sheffield University Management School, particularly Mr Robert Morgan, Dr Michael Kirk-Smith, Professor Arthur Meidan, Dr Anne Tomes, and Dr Anne Smith, who helped me with their comments, suggestions, and in other ways in the course of my development of multiple-choice questions for marketing. I am also indebted to Professor Luiz Moutinho of Cardiff University, for his very warm support of my efforts.

I must also thank the Management School's computing staff of Mrs Ann Jessop, Mrs Arleen Blackburn, and Mrs Diane Brook, as well as my tireless secretary, Miss Sharon Rose, for helping me over difficulties in producing the word-processed manuscript. My wife, Barbara, has to be thanked for her interest in the project and for providing me with the right conditions to get on with it. Last, I owe thanks to the many students who helped me to pre-test the questions.

Naturally, responsibility for any errors or shortcomings that, heaven forbid, are found in the text, is mine.

Everett M. Jacobs
Sheffield University Management School
November 1994

LIST OF ABBREVIATIONS

BCG	Boston Consulting Group
FLC	Family Life Cycle
GE	General Electric
JIT	Just-In-Time
PIMS	Profit Impact of Marketing Strategy
PLC	Product Life Cycle
PMP	Product Marketing Plan
SBU	Strategic Business Unit
SMP	Strategic Marketing Plan
SWOT	Strengths, Weaknesses, Opportunities, Threats
USP	Unique Selling Proposition
VMS	Vertical Marketing System

MARKETING STRATEGY

1.1
The management of Texas Instruments, the Dallas-based electronics firm, has historically had the strategic objective of perfecting mass production, bringing down costs, and cutting the price. This outlook reflects:

A   a selling orientation

B   a production orientation

C   a marketing orientation

D   a societal orientation

E   a product orientation

1.2*
France's Renault car company introduced a special edition 'Oasis' version of the 1.2 litre Clio RL Prima in the UK in autumn 1993. The advertising stressed that standard equipment included a new 'Watt' seat and door trim, unique wheel stylers, internally adjustable door mirrors, a tilt/slide sunroof, tinted glass, rear wash/wipe, an analogue clock, a folding rear seat, integral head restraints, opening rear quarter-lights, a 2×6 watt stereo radio/cassette player, Oasis graphics, the Renault anti-theft protection system, security window etching, a twelve-month unlimited mileage warranty, one year's free Royal Automobile Club membership, and an eight-year anti-corrosion warranty. The price of £6795 plus delivery was only about £200 more than the standard model, and was still among the least expensive cars in its class. The advertisement reflects:

A   a selling orientation

B   a production orientation

C   a marketing orientation

D   a societal orientation

E   a product orientation

1.3
The Campbell's Soup Company closely monitors all major storms moving across the United States in winter months, and advertises 'hot soup for cold weather' on local radio as the storm affects an area. This outlook reflects:

A   a selling orientation

B   a production orientation

C   a marketing orientation

D   a societal orientation

E   a product orientation

1.4
Which of the following **cannot** be considered an appropriate function of a marketing manager?

A   planning

B   organizing

C   controlling

D   appraising

E   selling

1.5*
The essential differences between marketing strategy and marketing tactics are that:

1   marketing strategy is long term, whereas marketing tactics are short term

2   marketing strategy is directed at the internal operation of the organization, whereas marketing tactics are directed at customers and competitors

3   strategic errors tend to have less effect than tactical errors on the organization

4   marketing strategy involves decisions about market segments to serve, product differential characteristics, and product positioning, whereas marketing tactics involve product, price, promotion, and distribution

5   marketing strategy is controlled by marketing organization management, whereas marketing tactics are controlled by marketing sub-unit management

A   1 and 2

B   1 and 3

C   2 and 3

D   3 and 4

E   4 and 5

1.6*

The correct strategic planning sequence for a multi-business company is to:

A develop a short -term marketing plan, followed by a strategic marketing plan, then a business unit marketing plan, and then a corporate marketing plan

B develop a strategic marketing plan, followed by a short-term marketing plan, then a business unit strategic plan, and then a corporate strategic plan

C develop a business unit strategic plan, followed by a corporate strategic plan, then a strategic marketing plan, and then a short-term marketing plan

D develop a corporate strategic plan, followed by a strategic marketing plan, then a short-term marketing plan, then a business unit strategic plan

E develop a corporate strategic plan, followed by a business unit strategic plan, then a strategic marketing plan, then a short-term marketing plan

1.7*

Which of the following statements does **not** correctly distinguish a Strategic Marketing Plan (SMP) from a Product Marketing Plan (PMP)?

A the SMP is concerned with corporate objectives, whereas the PMP is concerned only with marketing objectives

B the SMP implements product strategies by specifying how products are to be delivered and customers influenced, whereas the PMP allocates resources to carry out the product strategies

C the SMP is concerned with the company's overall product mix, whereas the PMP is concerned with the composition of the marketing mix

D the SMP integrates all corporate resources, whereas the PMP integrates only the marketing resources

E the SMP is the responsibility of top and strategic business unit (SBU) management, whereas the PMP is the responsibility of middle management

1.8

Which of the following objectives are normally considered to be **inappropriate** for a corporate mission statement?

1 the company aims to produce the highest-quality products and offer the best service to its customers

2 the company is committed to providing an environment for its employees that includes training and career development

3 the company is intent on increasing profits for its shareholders

4 the company will concentrate its activities on the South of England

5 the company will pursue a 'good neighbour' policy in areas where it operates, by supporting and participating in community events and programmes

A 1 and 2

B 1 and 3

C 2 and 3

D 3 and 4

E 4 and 5

1.9*

According to Ansoff's growth vector matrix, a corporate growth strategy based on market development seeks increased sales by:

A more aggressive promotion and distribution

B a market segmentation approach

C a product differentiation approach

D a combined market segmentation and product differentiation approach

E a heavy reliance on price

1.10*

According to Ansoff's growth vector matrix, a corporate growth strategy based on product development seeks increased sales by:

A more aggressive promotion and distribution

B a market segmentation approach

C a product differentiation approach

D a combined market segmentation and product differentiation approach

E a heavy reliance on price

1.11

In relation to the Ansoff growth vector matrix, the most important and most frequently used corporate development strategy is:

A product development

B market development

C market penetration

D diversification

E all the above are of equal weight

1.12

The riskiest and costliest of the corporate development options in the Ansoff growth vector matrix is normally:

A product development

B market development

C market penetration

D diversification

E all the above are of equal weight

1.13

In the Boston Consulting Group (BCG) approach to portfolio analysis, 'building' is an appropriate strategy:

A for weak cash cows from which more cash flow is needed

B for stars not likely to become market leaders

C for dogs generating losses and losing market share

D for strong cash cows if they are to continue to yield a large positive cash flow

E for question marks whose market shares have to grow if they are to become stars

1.14

In the BCG approach to portfolio analysis, 'holding' is an appropriate strategy:

A for weak cash cows from which more cash flow is needed

B for stars not likely to become market leaders

C for dogs generating losses and losing market share

D for strong cash cows if they are to continue to yield a large positive cash flow

E for question marks whose market shares have to grow if they are to become stars

1.15*

In the BCG approach to portfolio analysis, 'harvesting' is an appropriate strategy:

A for weak cash cows from which more cash flow is needed

B for stars not likely to become market leaders

C for dogs generating losses and losing market share

D for strong cash cows if they are to continue to yield a large positive cash flow

E for question marks whose market shares have to grow if they are to become stars

Case Study 1.1
Boston Consulting Group portfolio analysis

An industrial equipment company consists of the eight strategic business units (SBUs) shown in Table 1.1. Use the Boston Consulting Group portfolio analysis to answer questions 1.16–1.25. (*Note:* the line differentiating between market growth rates should be set at 10 per cent.)

Table 1.1
The strategic business units of Acme Industries Ltd

SBU	Sales (£m)	Number of competitors	Sales of top three (£m)	Market growth rate (%)
A	10	7	15, 15, 11	20
B	32	14	32, 16, 16	15
C	32	5	32, 8, 7	7
D	19	12	19, 18, 15	4
E	4	5	24, 19, 9	4
F	15	1	45, 15	1
G	12	5	24, 12, 12	11
H	84	10	84, 28, 27	13

1.16

The SBUs in the question mark (or problem child) category are:

A A and G

B A and B

C E and F

D C and D

E B and H

1.17

The SBUs in the star category are:

A A and G

B A and B

C E and F

D C and D

E B and H

1.18

The SBUs in the cash cow category are:

A A and G

B A and B

C E and F

D C and D

E B and H

1.19

The SBUs most in danger of moving into the dog category are:

A C and D

B D and E

C G and H

D D and G

E A and G

1.20

Which of the following SBUs has the weakest market position?

A C

B D

C E

D F

E G

1.21*

Which of the following SBUs has the strongest market position?

A A

B B

C C

D G

E H

1.22

For which of the following SBUs would a 'hold' objective be most appropriate?

A B

B C

C E

D G

E H

1.23

For which of the following SBUs would a 'build' objective be most appropriate?

A B

B D

C E

D F

E G

1.24

For which of the following SBUs would a 'harvest' objective be most appropriate?

A A

B B

C C

D D

E H

1.25

For which of the following SBUs would a 'divest' objective be most appropriate?

A A

B C

C E

D G

E H

1.26*

Which of the following are **invalid** as criticisms of the BCG matrix?

1 principally because of the product life-cycle (PLC) effect, SBUs will change their position on the matrix without company action

2 the graphic illustration of cash flows is applicable to only a limited number of markets, particularly where growth is relatively high and a definite pattern of PLCs can be observed

3 not all question marks (problem children) can be turned into stars

4 one of the key assumptions of the BCG matrix, that higher rates of market share are associated with higher profit rates, may not always be true

5 the milking of cash cows to fund new products may put the position of some or all of the cash cows in jeopardy

A 1 and 2

B 1 and 3

C 2 and 3

D 3 and 4

E 4 and 5

1.27*

Which of the following is an **inaccurate** comparison between the BCG and the McKinsey/General Electric (GE) approach?

A the plotted circles on the BCG grid depict the size of the company's business, whereas those on the GE grid depict the size of the relevant market

B the BCG factor of market growth is subsumed under the GE variable of market attractiveness

C placement of the dividing line between high and low market growth in the BCG matrix is determined objectively, whereas the division of the GE matrix into high/strong, medium, and low/weak segments is determined subjectively

D it is more difficult to define an SBU in the BCG approach than in the GE approach

E the GE approach is much more complex than the BCG approach, and requires much more extensive data gathering and processing

1.28*
Which of the following are **invalid** as criticisms of the GE approach?

1 there is a limit to the number of factors that can be used to assess market attractiveness or competitive position

2 there is no precise indication as to how to weight the various elements of market attractiveness, or how to score business strengths against these

3 management's role is too limited in the GE approach

4 evaluation and scoring is subjective

5 the GE approach is not supported by empirical evidence or research

A 1 and 2

B 1 and 3

C 2 and 3

D 3 and 4

E 4 and 5

1.29
In the GE matrix, the recommended strategy for an SBU assigned to the cell indicating strong competitive position and high market attractiveness should be to:

A specialize around existing strengths, but ultimately withdraw if indications of substantial growth are lacking

B defend strengths, concentrate on attractive segments, and manage for current earnings

C protect the existing programme, and selectively concentrate investments in segments where earnings are good and risk is relatively low

D concentrate effort on maintaining strength, and invest to grow at the maximum desirable rate

E cut fixed costs and avoid investment while preparing to sell at a time that will maximize cash value

1.30
In the GE matrix, the recommended strategy for an SBU assigned to the cell indicating medium competitive position and medium market attractiveness is to:

A specialize around existing strengths, but ultimately withdraw if indications of substantial growth are lacking

B defend strengths, concentrate on attractive segments, and manage for current earnings

C protect the existing programme, and selectively concentrate investments in segments where earnings are good and risk is relatively low

D concentrate effort on maintaining strength, and invest to grow at the maximum desirable rate

E cut fixed costs and avoid investment while preparing to sell at a time that will maximize cash value

1.31
In the GE matrix, the recommended strategy for an SBU assigned to the cell indicating weak competitive position and low market attractiveness is to:

A specialize around existing strengths, but ultimately withdraw if indications of substantial growth are lacking

B defend strengths, concentrate on attractive segments, and manage for current earnings

C protect the existing programme, and selectively concentrate investments in segments where earnings are good and risk is relatively low

D concentrate effort on maintaining strength, and invest to grow at the maximum desirable rate

E cut fixed costs and avoid investment while preparing to sell at a time that will maximize cash value

1.32
In the analysis of strengths, weaknesses, opportunities and threats (SWOT analysis), which of the following are **not** covered in the internal analysis?

1 mission and objectives

2 financial resources

3 environmental scanning

4 products

5 performance trends

A 1 and 2
B 1 and 3
C 2 and 3
D 3 and 4
E 4 and 5

1.33*

A company carrying out a SWOT analysis has drawn up a list of fifteen strengths, two weaknesses, four opportunities, and one threat. In order to interpret the list, it is necessary to:

1 determine the importance of, or weight to attach to, each item on the list

2 find more weaknesses and threats in order to provide balance

3 ascertain the company's priorities before interpreting the list

4 isolate the key issues that will be important to the future of the company

5 question whether the strengths were identified objectively

A 1 and 2
B 1 and 3
C 2 and 3
D 3 and 4
E 4 and 5

1.34

Which of the following information is **not** provided to parent companies in profit impact of marketing strategy (PIMS) reports on the companies' businesses (i.e. divisions, product lines, or other profit centres)?

A an overall assessment of the impact of future changes in the market on business strategy

B a report on the return on investment (ROI) that is normal for the type of business

C a computational prediction of the normal short- and long-term consequences of several possible strategic moves in the business

D a report indicating the best combination of several strategies that promises to give optimal results for the business

E an examination of possible tactics for achieving strategic objectives, based on a close analysis of strategically similar businesses

1.35

Which is the 'odd one out' of the following markets?

A need markets

B demographic markets

C voter markets

D product markets

E geographic markets

1.36

A potential market is the group of consumers who:

A have interest in a defined market offer

B have sufficient income to purchase a defined market offer

C have access to a particular market offer

D have interest, income, and access to a particular market offer

E have already bought the market offer

1.37

Which of the following information is **not** required by a company to estimate total market demand?

A definition of the marketing environment

B definition of customer group

C determination of company's volume of sales in physical or monetary terms

D specification of time period

E specification of product or service

1.38*

In investigating whether to select a market for entry or expansion, which of the following sought characteristics may exhibit a trade-off relationship?

1 an increasing share of market for the brand

2 good potential for market growth

3 no need for significant capital investment

4 ease of entry and competitive vulnerability

5 stability in market demand

A 1 and 2
B 1 and 3
C 2 and 3
D 3 and 4
E 4 and 5

1.39

When an organization attempts to encourage a want for an object in people who initially have no knowledge or interest in the object, it is engaging in:

A conversional marketing

B stimulational marketing

C developmental marketing

D maintenance marketing

E remarketing

1.40

When an organization attempts to defend the existing level of sales against competitive forces, it is engaging in:

A conversional marketing

B stimulational marketing

C developmental marketing

D maintenance marketing

E remarketing

1.41

When an organization attempts to rebuild interest in a stable or declining product or service, it is engaging in:

A conversional marketing

B stimulational marketing

C developmental marketing

D maintenance marketing

E remarketing

1.42*

The difference between demarketing and countermarketing is that:

A demarketing tries to alter the time pattern of demand, whereas countermarketing attempts to get people who dislike something to like it

B demarketing attempts to get people who dislike something to like it, whereas countermarketing tries to alter the time pattern of demand

C demarketing attempts to reduce the demand for a product or service on a temporary or permanent basis, whereas countermarketing attempts to destroy the demand or interest in a particular product or service

D demarketing attempts to destroy the demand or interest in a particular product or service, whereas countermarketing tries to reduce the demand for a product or service on a temporary or permanent basis

E none of these

1.43*

Which of the following statements **inaccurately** characterize the marketing mix?

1 a firm should adjust its marketing mix variables every six months

2 the customer is part of the marketing mix

3 each targeted market requires a separate marketing mix

4 in the four-factor classification of marketing mix tools, all the factors are equally important

5 there is only one best way to mix marketing variables

A 1 and 2

B 1 and 3

C 2 and 3

D 3 and 4

E 4 and 5

1.44

The Sheffield Steelers, a professional ice hockey team in the British Premier Division, began a publicity and advertising campaign in local newspapers near the start of August 1994 in anticipation of the first game of the season on 11 September. People telephoning the box office were unexpectedly told that they could not order tickets until 28 August, causing considerable annoyance in some cases. The situation indicates a fault in which part(s) of the Steelers' marketing mix?

A product alone

B place alone

C promotion alone

D place and promotion

E product and promotion

1.45*

The preferred marketing mix strategy for staple goods is to:

A gain adequate representation in major shopping districts or large shopping centres

B gain widespread distribution at low cost

C distribute the product through a limited number of outlets

D promote the product through aggressive personal selling

E emphasize low price

1.46*

The preferred marketing mix strategy for unsought products is to:

A gain adequate representation in major shopping districts or large shopping centres

B gain widespread distribution at low cost

C distribute the product through a limited number of outlets

D promote the product through aggressive personal selling

E emphasize low price

1.47*

The difference between internal marketing and external marketing is that:

A internal marketing refers to the direct link between the organization and its employees, whereas external marketing refers to the direct link between the organization and its customers

B internal marketing refers to the direct link between the organization and its employees, whereas external marketing refers to the direct link between the organization's employees and its customers

C internal marketing refers to the direct link between the organization's employees and its customers, whereas external marketing refers to the direct link between the organization and its customers

D internal marketing refers to the direct link between the organization's employees and its customers, whereas external marketing refers to the direct link between the organization and its employees

E none of these

1.48*

Which of the following is **not** a purpose of a marketing audit?

A describing current activities and results related to sales, costs, prices, profits, and other performance feedbacks

B gathering information about customers, competition, and environmental developments that may affect marketing strategy

C exploring opportunities and alternatives for improving the marketing strategy

D assessing how well the firm has implemented its marketing strategy, achieved its objectives, and allocated its resources

E providing an overall database to be used in evaluating the attainment of organizational goals and marketing objectives

1.49

In which of the following functional audits should management be informed whether the customers see the company's prices as being in line with the value of its offer?

A marketing strategy audit

B marketing systems audit

C marketing function audit

D marketing organization audit

E marketing productivity audit

1.50*

Which of the following statements correctly indicates the position of the marketing audit in the control of the marketing organization?

A the marketing audit is external to the control of marketing performance

B the marketing audit may be used in after-the-fact control, in steering control, or in adaptive control

C the marketing audit may be used in after-the-fact control but not in steering control or in adaptive control

D the marketing audit may be used in steering control, but not in after-the-fact control or in adaptive control

E the marketing audit may be used in adaptive control, but not in after-the-fact control or in steering control

2

SEGMENTATION AND POSITIONING

2.1*

Which of the following statements **incorrectly** distinguishes between market aggregation (product differentiation) and market segmentation?

A market aggregation is most economical when consumer needs are relatively homogeneous, whereas market segmentation is most economical when consumer needs are highly heterogeneous

B with market aggregation, the firm maximizes profits by selling one or a few products to a mass market, whereas with market segmentation, specific products are aimed at defined segments

C with market aggregation, the main thrust of marketing strategy is to differentiate the company's single product from competitive brands by product attributes, heavy advertising, and lower price, whereas with market segmentation, the main thrust of marketing strategy is based on market differentiation, by developing unique products to meet the needs of market segments

D with market aggregation, the limits to profit maximization are the additional advertising and other marketing costs required to keep up with the competition, whereas with market segmentation, the limits to profit maximization are the additional costs required to develop and market new products for additional market segments

E with market aggregation, profit maximization is through increases in advertising expenditure, whereas with market segmentation, profit maximization is through economies of scale in production and marketing

2.2

Undifferentiated marketing is an appropriate strategy when:

1 the market has been developed for a number of years
2 there is little variation in the needs of customers for a specific product

3 cost economies are of great importance to the organization
4 the organization wishes to minimize competition
5 the market can be satisfied with a single marketing mix

A 1 and 2
B 1 and 3
C 2 and 3
D 3 and 4
E 4 and 5

2.3

Which of the following statements **incorrectly** compares differentiated marketing with undifferentiated marketing?

A vulnerability to competition is usually greater with differentiated marketing

B production costs for the same total output are usually higher for differentiated marketing

C inventory costs for the same total output are usually higher for differentiated marketing

D product development costs are usually higher for differentiated marketing

E the marketing channels are usually more diverse for differentiated marketing

2.4

Which of the following pairs of products do **not** belong to the same product market?

A Pizza Hut pizza, McDonald's hamburger

B live performance of the opera *Aida*, filmed version of Shakespeare's *Hamlet*

C motorized wheelchair, family car

D digital watch, analogue watch

E a baseball bat, a football

2.5*

In terms of product markets, Maxwell House decaffeinated instant coffee represents a:

A product variant

B single-level designation

C brand product-market

D product-type product-market

E generic product-market

2.6

Which of the following is **not** part of the customer profiling procedure?

A identifying buyer decision criteria

B identifying who are the existing/potential customers

C identifying what external/environmental factors influence buying

D identifying what company marketing efforts the customers require

E describing the characteristics of the customers

2.7

When a firm targets some segments of a market and provides a different product for each, it is employing a strategy of:

A concentrated marketing

B selective specialization

C market specialization

D product specialization

E full coverage

2.8

When a firm targets some segments of a market and provides only one product for all of them, it is employing a strategy of:

A concentrated marketing

B selective specialization

C market specialization

D product specialization

E full coverage

2.9

A low market share company should **avoid** which strategy of target market selection?

A concentrated marketing

B selective specialization

C market specialization

D product specialization

E full coverage

2.10*

Which criteria are **not necessarily** required for the effective segmentation of a market?

1 using a single variable to segment the market

2 ensuring heterogeneity between segments

3 constructing each segment so as to maximize profitability

4 ensuring the stability of each segment

5 ensuring the accessibility of each segment

A 1 and 2

B 1 and 3

C 2 and 3

D 3 and 4

E 4 and 5

2.11

A manufacturer has identified four customer groups: men aged 20–35; men aged 36–50; women aged 20–35; women aged 36–50. Initial market research has indicated that most people in the four groups rate the quality of a new product in the range of good–very good–excellent. The manufacturer should:

A redefine the customer groups to test the validity of the findings before deciding whether to market the product

B immediately market the product without alteration

C improve product quality and re-test before deciding whether to market the product

D test other variables before deciding whether to market the product

E develop and test another product, and compare the results with the first product, before deciding whether to market either

2.12*

A particular market has been divided into six segments. In devising a segmentation strategy, a manufacturer should:

1 target the largest segment

2 use a different marketing mix for each targeted segment

3 ensure the behavioural relevance of the basis of segmentation

4 target the most accessible segment

5 appraise the impact on long-term profitability of targeting any segment

A 1 and 2

B 1 and 3

C 2 and 3

D 3 and 4

E 4 and 5

2.13*

Counter-segmentation, or the consolidation of several segments into one large segment, may be an appropriate objective when:

1 the reduction in costs exceeds the reduction in profits

2 consumers show reduced price sensitivity

3 the similarities among potential customers outweigh differences

4 it is too expensive for a company to launch a new product

5 the demand curves for the segments to be combined are similar

A 1 and 2

B 1 and 3

C 2 and 3

D 3 and 4

E 4 and 5

2.14

An important difference between psychographic and behavioural variables used to segment consumer markets is that:

A psychographic variables cannot be quantified, whereas behavioural variables can

B psychographic variables refer to consumer characteristics, whereas behavioural variables refer to consumer responses

C psychographic variables refer to consumer responses, whereas behavioural variables refer to consumer characteristics

D psychographic variables can be related to demographic variables, whereas behavioural variables cannot

E psychographic variables cannot be related to demographic variables, whereas behavioural variables can

2.15

Which of the following segmentation variables is the 'odd one out'?

A occupation

B social class

C education

D income

E family size

2.16

Which of the following has **not** been a characteristic of demographic change in the United States, Britain, and Western Europe throughout the 1980s?

A an increase in mobility

B an increase in the proportion of teenagers in the population

C an increase in the proportion of retired people in the population

D a decline in the birthrate

E an increase in the proportion of women in the workforce

2.17

Which of the following are appropriate bases for geodemographic segmentation?

1 city size

2 state, county, or province

3 population density

4 postal code

5 classification of residential neighbourhoods

A 1 and 2

B 1 and 3

C 2 and 3

D 3 and 4

E 4 and 5

2.18*

Which of the following statements about usage segmentation is **incorrect**?

A demographic characteristics are generally poor predictors of heavy usage

B for almost all consumer product categories, the top 50 per cent of users account for 80–90 per cent of total volume

C heavy usage of one product category is relatively independent of heavy usage of another

D heavy users usually exhibit more brand loyalty than light users

E heavy users tend to pay as much, or even a little more, for a unit of purchase than do light users

2.19*

The combination of social class and income as a segmentation variable is generally superior to the use of social class or income alone for which of these products?

A clothing

B washing machines

C imported wines

D frozen food

E kitchen waste disposal

2.20

Which of the following characteristics are **not** normally employed to define subcultures for segmentation purposes?

1 education

2 age

3 geography

4 family life cycle

5 income

A 1 and 2

B 1 and 3

C 2 and 3

D 3 and 4

E 4 and 5

2.21*

Although the 'Hispanic market' in the United States is not homogeneous, being composed of consumers of different national identities, its description as a subculture for segmentation purposes is justified because:

A the group is quite large (almost 10 per cent of the United States population) and has significant purchasing power (over $50 billion annually at the end of the 1980s)

B the group's linguistic homogeneity overrides diversity in national identities and distinguishes it from other consumers

C the group's adherence to certain traditional values distinguishes it from other consumers

D the group's purchase behaviour and preferences distinguish it from other consumers

E the group's choice of media distinguishes it from other consumers

2.22

Which of the following criticisms is **incorrect** regarding the use of personality traits as a means of market segmentation?

A studies suggest only a weak relationship between personality variables and purchase variables

B personality theory has only limited capability to explain the low involvement decisions typical of day-to-day consumer behaviour

C people can show different personality profiles and yet still prefer basically the same product attributes

D unless people with common personality dimensions are homogeneous in terms of such factors as age, income, or location, they cannot be reached economically through the mass media

E personality traits are too unstable to be used in market segmentation

2.23*

Benefit segmentation differs from volume segmentation in that:

1 benefit segmentation measures consumer value systems whereas volume segmentation measures consumption

2 benefit segmentation indicates precisely why a customer has bought a product, whereas volume segmentation does not

3 benefit segmentation data are operationally easier to generate than volume segmentation data

4 benefit segmentation is useful for predicting brand preference, whereas volume segmentation is not

5 benefit segmentation relies on causal factors, whereas volume segmentation relies on descriptive factors

A 1 and 2

B 1 and 3

C 2 and 3

D 3 and 4

E 4 and 5

2.24

Which of the following characteristics **incorrectly** describe benefit segmentation?

1 it is based on measuring consumer value systems

2 it is based on *ex post facto* analysis of consumers making up various market segments

3 it relies on descriptive factors

4 it seeks to identify distinct consumer needs

5 it relies on causal factors

A 1 and 2
B 1 and 3
C 2 and 3
D 3 and 4
E 4 and 5

2.25*

Which of the following statements about lifestyle segmentation are correct?

1 it is quite rare for people to change their lifestyle
2 a lifestyle segmentation strategy cannot be combined with any other segmentation strategy
3 there is no agreement about a standard set of lifestyle categories
4 psychographic variables used to measure lifestyle are more difficult to measure accurately than other types of segmentation variables
5 lifestyle segmentation is inappropriate for predicting brand preference

A 1 and 2
B 1 and 3
C 2 and 3
D 3 and 4
E 4 and 5

2.26*

Which of the following characteristics are **not** usually used for lifestyle segmentation?

1 social class
2 religion
3 interests
4 activities
5 opinions

A 1 and 2
B 1 and 3
C 2 and 3
D 3 and 4
E 4 and 5

2.27

If a department store finds that a major characteristic of its customers is their desire for more leisure, it would be well advised to consider:

1 emphasizing product quality
2 developing mail order shopping

3 introducing Freephone telephone ordering of merchandise
4 upgrading its in-store décor
5 opening a crèche/kindergarten to supervise under-fives while their parent(s) shop

A 1 and 2
B 1 and 3
C 2 and 3
D 3 and 4
E 4 and 5

2.28

Which of the following criticisms of age as a segmentation variable is **invalid**?

A age is a poor predictor of a person's health, work status, or family status
B chronological age is not necessarily synonymous with psychological age
C age is not an accurate predictor of a person's spending habits
D the similarities in consumer wants for different age groups are often greater than the differences
E age is not a reliable predictor of lifestyle

2.29

Which of the following is **not** an essential part of effective positioning strategy?

A determining what is value to the target customers
B developing products with numerous product differences compared with competing brands
C choosing a price strategy
D selecting an image that differentiates the product from competing products
E determining target customers' needs

2.30

BMW's slogan 'the ultimate driving machine' reflects a strategy of positioning:

A by attribute or product feature
B by use or application
C by product user
D by competitor
E by problem solution or needs

2.31

Which of the following statements represents the correct sequence for developing a marketing strategy?

A select a target market, develop a marketing mix, determine a positioning strategy

B determine a positioning strategy, develop a marketing mix, select a target market

C select a target market, determine a positioning strategy, develop a marketing mix

D determine a positioning strategy, select a target market, develop a marketing mix

E develop a marketing mix, determine a positioning strategy, select a target market

2.32

Which of the following is **not** usually considered a useful basis for constructing a positioning strategy?

A positioning on specific product features

B positioning on benefits

C positioning for an undifferentiated market

D positioning for usage occasions

E positioning for user category

2.33

A brand's competitive positioning relates to:

A its price relative to other brands

B its product features relative to other brands

C the way the industry perceives it relative to the competition

D its market share

E the way consumers perceive it relative to the competition

2.34*

In an advertisement claiming that McDonald's hamburgers had less beef and did not taste as good as Burger King's because McDonald's were not flame-grilled, Burger King was attempting to:

1 join an exclusive club in the minds of the target customers

2 deposition or reposition the competition

3 secure a previously unoccupied market position that is valued by the target customers

4 strengthen its own current position in the minds of target customers

5 change the product attributes and psychological positioning of its product

A 1 and 2

B 1 and 3

C 2 and 3

D 3 and 4

E 4 and 5

2.35*

We can deduce from the perceptual map in Figure 2.1 that:

A there is no room in the market for another restaurant

B the ideal restaurant, as perceived by the consumers, would be positioned outside the boxed area

C restaurant 4 is more profitable than restaurant 3

D there would be demand for a new restaurant positioned somewhere in the boxed area

E a new restaurant wanting to position itself on the high-quality side of the boxed area should develop variables apart from price and quality

2.36

The restaurants in greatest competition in Figure 2.1 are:

A 3 and 5

B 9 and 10

C 7 and 8

D 6 and 8

E cannot be determined

2.37

It is **inappropriate** to reposition a brand:

A if it begins to lose market share

B when consumer preferences change

C if the original positioning loses its distinctiveness

D on a frequent basis

E when it progresses to a different stage of the product life cycle

2.38

Which of the following would **not** be used to reposition a brand?

A a new brand name

B the addition of a new product feature

C a change in the channel of distribution

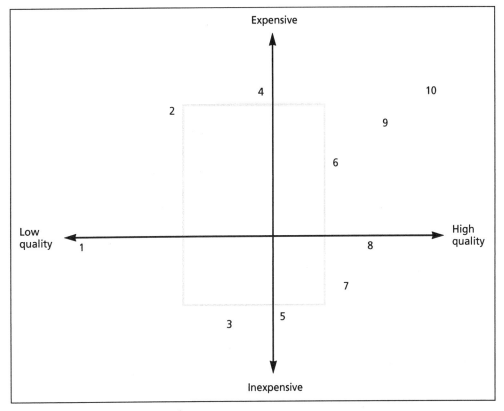

Fig. 2.1 Consumer perception of ten restaurants

D a change in the person advocating the brand in an advertisement

E the distribution of limited-period money-off coupons

2.39*
A company's range of cutlery extends from moderately priced good-quality stainless steel to luxury sterling silver, but it is generally known for only the latter. This situation reflects:

A repositioning

B overpositioning

C underpositioning

D confused positioning

E doubtful positioning

2.40*
A store selling fine Waterford Glass glass vases at £100 and Bohemian glass vases of comparable size and quality at £40 finds that some customers believe the Bohemian products are imperfect. This situation reflects:

A repositioning

B overpositioning

C underpositioning

D confused positioning

E doubtful positioning

2.41*
Positioning to avoid competition may be best when:

1 A firm introduces a brand into a market in which it already has one or more brands

2 the product is priced lower than competing brands

3 the product's performance characteristics are not significantly different from competing brands

4 the brand has unique characteristics that are important to some buyers

5 the product is priced higher than competing brands

A 1 and 2

B 1 and 3

C 2 and 3

D 3 and 4

E 4 and 5

Case Study 2.1
Heavy-duty floor cleaner

A heavy-duty floor cleaner was positioned to empha-size its ability to remove dirt. However, recent lifestyle research showed that the target segment was becom-ing more concerned with cleanliness from the stand-point of health rather than utilitarian housekeeping benefits. Consumer research also showed that a signif-icant proportion of present customers used the floor cleaner to clean toilets (12 per cent) and to keep sink and bath drains smelling sweet (7 per cent).

Questions 2.42–2.46 relate to this case study

2.42

The best strategy in terms of product positioning is to:

A make no changes

B partially reposition the product to emphasize dis-infectant properties

C completely reposition the product to emphasize health properties

D completely reposition the product to emphasize gen-eral cleaning properties

E none of these

2.43*

The best strategy in terms of product development for the cleaner would be to:

A make no changes

B change the packaging

C change the smell

D conduct further research to find out why lifestyles are changing

E conduct further research to construct a consumers' perceptual map

2.44*

In terms of advertising, which of the following themes would be **inappropriate** for the cleaner?

A a woman using the cleaner in a sports centre show-er room

B two women discussing how quickly 'Jim's mess from the garden' came off the kitchen floor

C a young woman cleaning a toilet bowl with the product

D a well-known television personality holding a bot-tle of the cleaner and saying, 'It meets *my* standards'

E none of these

2.45

In terms of price, the manufacturer's best strategy to encourage trials is to:

A raise the price, but give a free gift with purchase

B maintain the price, but have widespread advertising

C maintain the price, but give money off for a set period

D maintain the price, but give money back for five proofs of purchase

E maintain the price, but give 20 per cent extra free for a set period

2.46*

Following from the unexpected uses uncovered in the research, the manufacturer is best advised to consider:

A listing all current uses on the product label

B developing a new product for sink and bath drains and toilets

C developing a new product only for toilets

D developing a new product for toilets, and another for sink and bath drains

E warning against misuse of the product

Case Study 2.2
Kellogg's Bran Flakes

At the end of the 1980s, a Kellogg's Bran Flakes televi-sion advertisement in Britain featured a young, pre-sumably married, couple dressed in similar colourful jogging suits, singing a catchy tune about the product. The husband and wife alternated lines, and both mimed to the voice of a male. The chorus was, 'They're tasty, tasty, very very tasty; they're very tasty'. The adver-tisement ended with about one dozen similarly dressed couples joining in the chorus.

In 1993, an advertisement for Kellogg's Bran Flakes featured a father and his teenage son talking at the breakfast table on the patio. The son expressed surprise at the father's jogging suit, and mild astonishment that the father was eating Kellogg's Bran Flakes. The father explained that the product was high in fibre, low in fat, and was part of 'a new healthier lifestyle'. A 'voice over' commented that the product was 'a step in the right direction'.

Questions 2.47–2.50 relate to this case study

2.47*

At whom was the purchasing message directed in the 1980s advertisement?

A husbands and wives of all ages

B young husbands and wives

C older husbands and wives

D husbands alone

E wives alone

2.48*

The implied main marketing strategy in the 1980s advertisement was:

A changing the usage situation

B encouraging a switch

C counter-segmentation

D lifestyle segmentation

E repositioning the product

2.49*

The implied target market in the 1993 advertisement was:

A adult men (18+)

B adult women (18+)

C all adults

D only middle-aged adults

E all cereal consumers, regardless of age

2.50*

The implied main marketing strategy in the 1993 advertisement was:

A changing the usage situation

B encouraging a switch

C counter-segmentation

D lifestyle segmentation

E repositioning the product

3

CONSUMER BEHAVIOUR

3.1
The affective component of attitudes is represented by:

A buying intention

B needs

C past experience with the brand

D verbal praise of the brand

E positive or negative feelings about the brand

3.2
The cognitive component of attitudes is represented by:

A buying intention

B needs

C past experience with the brand

D verbal praise of the brand

E positive or negative feelings about the brand

3.3
Post-purchase dissonance in relation to a product can be reduced by which of the following means?

1 selectively interpreting negative information positively

2 decreasing the level of prior expectation of product performance

3 engaging in symbolic purchase evaluation

4 seeking reassurance from someone else who bought the product

5 seeking advertisements featuring competing brands

A 1 and 2

B 1 and 3

C 2 and 3

D 3 and 4

E 4 and 5

3.4*
A contrast effect is likely to lead a consumer to:

1 search more for positive information about the brand

2 interpret negative information about the brand more negatively

3 ignore positive information about the brand

4 decrease levels of prior expectation of product performance

5 ignore negative information about the brand

A 1 and 2

B 1 and 3

C 2 and 3

D 3 and 4

E 4 and 5

3.5
In contrast to extended problem-solving, limited problem-solving is characterized by which of the following?

1 beliefs, attitudes, and intentions are less strongly held

2 absence of recognized needs

3 less time spent in selection

4 greater use of friends for information

5 less product evaluation before purchase

A 1 and 2

B 1 and 3

C 2 and 3

D 3 and 4

E 4 and 5

3.6*
In contrast to extended problem-solving, habitual purchasing behaviour is characterized by which of the following?

1 strong brand attitudes

2 greater need for social approval of purchase

3 external stimuli more important

4 more structured need priorities

5 consumer is more likely to be confident in choice

A 1 and 2
B 1 and 3
C 2 and 3
D 3 and 4
E 4 and 5

3.7*
In contrast to extended problem-solving, habitual purchasing behaviour is characterized by which of the following?

1 greater degree of selective perception
2 stimuli tend to be ambiguous
3 limited information search
4 more time between intention and purchase
5 high frequency of purchase

A 1 and 2
B 1 and 3
C 2 and 3
D 3 and 4
E 4 and 5

3.8
Which of the following strategies by marketers challenging the brand leader is most likely to induce consumers to switch from habit to decision-making?

1 increasing price of existing brand
2 introducing a new feature in existing brand
3 using free product samples
4 concentrating distribution in fewer outlets
5 using discount coupons

A 1 and 2
B 1 and 3
C 2 and 3
D 3 and 4
E 4 and 5

3.9
Products whose purchase is characterized by habit are more likely to:

A use in-store stimuli to influence people
B use advertising to convey information
C be visible products
D use advertising to stimulate pre-purchase deliberation
E rely on price deals

3.10*
Which of the following advertising and promotional themes attempt to apply classical conditioning?

1 Tina Turner drinking Pepsi-Cola
2 a BMW suspended by its doors
3 Black & Decker hammer drill making a hole in concrete
4 the Marlboro cowboy campaign
5 Budweiser beer sponsoring American football on British television

A 1 and 2
B 1 and 3
C 2 and 3
D 3 and 4
E 4 and 5

3.11*
Which of the following advertising and promotional themes attempt to apply instrumental conditioning?

1 Tina Turner drinking Pepsi-Cola
2 a BMW suspended by its doors
3 Black & Decker hammer drill making a hole in concrete
4 the Marlboro cowboy campaign
5 Budweiser beer sponsoring American football on British television

A 1 and 2
B 1 and 3
C 2 and 3
D 3 and 4
E 4 and 5

3.12*
Corrective advertising seeks to eliminate any link between deceptive advertising and consumer beliefs through:

A forgetting
B repetition
C extinction
D reinforcement
E contiguity

3.13*
Brand loyalty is more likely to occur when the brand is:

A well known

B a private brand

C a durable good

D a low-involvement purchase

E not seen as risky

3.14*
Behavioural measures have defined brand loyalty by:

A sequence of purchases of a certain brand

B brand attitudes

C future purchase intent

D the number of consumers who have bought the brand

E the brand's market share over a period of time

3.15
Brand-loyal consumers, compared with those showing little brand loyalty, are more likely to be:

A opinion leaders

B younger

C innovators

D less interested in status

E store loyal

3.16
Consumer involvement with a brand or product relates to:

A a perception of the brand or product

B the degree of personal importance ascribed to the brand or product

C regular purchase of the brand or product

D brand or product satisfaction

E the decision to favour one brand over another

3.17
Consumers are more likely to be involved in a decision when:

A the product is frequently purchased

B the product is expected to provide pleasure

C purchase entails significant risks

D the product is bought for oneself rather than for the family

E social pressures are felt

3.18
In low-involvement decisions:

A consumers are information seekers

B consumers' lifestyle characteristics are related to purchase behaviour

C consumers' attitudes are related to behaviour

D consumers seek an acceptable level of satisfaction

E consumers are information processors

3.19*
Which of the following products are likely to be high-involvement goods?

1 blue jeans

2 beer

3 soap

4 personal stereo

5 calculator battery

A 1 and 2

B 1 and 3

C 2 and 3

D 3 and 4

E 4 and 5

3.20
Buying by inertia generally involves:

A high involvement and significant differences between brands

B high involvement and few differences between brands

C low involvement and significant differences between brands

D low involvement and few differences between brands

E none of the above

3.21
Perception is a selective process that is directed by:

A social influences on the consumer

B a consumer's current predisposition and attitudes

C advertising

D past consumer perceptions

E product pricing

3.22
Stimuli are more likely to be perceived when they:

A conform to cultural norms

B are complex

C deal with information about existing brands

D contradict the consumer's beliefs and experiences

E relate to consumer needs

3.23*
The basic process of consumer perception requires:

A dissonance reduction

B communication

C evaluation

D conflict resolution

E organization

3.24*
Which of the following is **not** involved in the process of selective perception?

A selective exposure

B selective attention

C selective comprehension

D selective retention

E selective intention

3.25*
Consumers are most likely to associate higher prices with higher quality when:

A criteria of product performance are lacking

B the brand has a definite image

C it is a new product

D the manufacturer is well known

E perceived risk in purchasing the product is high

3.26
A marketing strategy meant to reduce the consequences of product failure is:

A money-back guarantees

B expert testimonials

C providing more information

D increasing the number of outlets carrying the product

E all of the above

3.27*
The importance of attitudes in determining subsequent behaviour tends to be emphasized most by:

A classical learning theory

B cognitive dissonance

C theory of social judgement

D passive learning

E the hierarchy of effects

3.28
The Right Guard deodorant advertising theme, 'Hands up if you use Right Guard, hands down if you don't', is directed towards which attitude function as defined by Katz?

A utilitarian

B ego-defensive

C beliefs

D organization of knowledge

E value-expressive

3.29
McDonald's advertising theme, 'You deserve a break today', is directed towards which attitude function as defined by Katz?

A utilitarian

B ego-defensive

C beliefs

D organization of knowledge

E value-expressive

3.30*
Multi-attribute models do **not** provide a means of identifying:

A the strengths and weaknesses of a brand relative to competition

B the needs of consumer segments based on what they consider important or desirable

C the association between brand attitudes and consumer demographic and lifestyle characteristics

D brand attitudes most closely related to overall attitudes towards the brand and intention to buy

E new product opportunities based on unmet consumer needs

3.31*

Which of the following does **not** represent a strategy of attitude change based on multi-attribute models?

A link the brand to an involving situation or issue

B change brand beliefs

C change the direction of consumer needs

D add a new attribute to increase the attractiveness of the brand

E change the intensity of consumer needs

3.32*

A good strategy to induce attitude-discrepant behaviour is to:

A increase the warranty period of the brand

B change the package design

C introduce a new product attribute

D lower the price of the brand

E link the brand to an involving situation or issue

3.33

Research has indicated that coupon-induced triers were less likely to repurchase the product than those who tried the product without the coupon inducement. This finding suggests that:

1 coupons should not be used in trying to change purchase behaviour

2 coupon users tend to be more brand loyal than non-users

3 one-off incentives may be inadequate for modifying long-term behaviour

4 removal of deal-based incentives may lead to the extinction of purchase behaviour

5 product involvement is more important than coupons in encouraging repurchase

A 1 and 2

B 1 and 3

C 2 and 3

D 3 and 4

E 4 and 5

3.34*

Which of the following **fails** to explain adequately why it is difficult to use attitude to predict behaviour or behaviour change?

A there are problems in defining and measuring attitudes

B attitudes can be influenced by overt behaviour

C any given attitude may give rise to a variety of behaviours

D intervening factors may make it impossible to behave consistently with attitude

E negative attitude does not always result in negative behaviour

3.35

The individual who has the role of influencing the type of stimuli the decision unit is exposed to is known as the:

A influencer

B decision-maker

C information-gatherer

D purchasing agent

E consumer

3.36*

The process by which, in many cases, joint decisions lead to riskier choices than individual decisions is known as:

A perceived risk

B shared risk

C risk shift

D functional risk

E risk-oriented decision-making

3.37*

The least constructive form of conflict resolution in family decision-making is:

A bargaining

B problem-solving

C consensus

D coalitions

E role specialization

3.38*

Conflict in family decision-making over a purchase is least probable when only one family member:

A collects information

B evaluates alternative brands

C assesses purchase risk

D is going to pay for the purchase

E shows purchase involvement

3.39

Research by an appliance manufacturer indicated that spouses/partners in the target market frequently disagreed over the relative importance of performance and economy. It would therefore be most advisable for the manufacturer to:

A choose a target market where there is a consensus on the importance of performance and economy

B emphasize extra features at the expense of economy

C emphasize economy at the expense of extra features

D offer a complete product line ranging from a stripped-down basic model to an ultra-deluxe model

E develop one brand for males and another for females

3.40*

A large fast-food chain has been running two television advertisements, one showing children aged 4–10 enjoying its products and one showing people aged 15–30 enjoying its products. A switch to a new advertisement portraying a family of five enjoying the products would probably:

A cause overall sales to rise

B cause overall sales to drop

C cause children's sales to drop

D cause adults' sales to drop

E none of these

3.41

Which of the following final purchase decisions are most likely to be syncratic?

1 non-prescription drugs
2 garden plants
3 vacations
4 outside entertainment
5 child's clothing

A 1 and 2
B 1 and 3
C 2 and 3
D 3 and 4
E 4 and 5

3.42

Which of the following final purchase decisions are most likely to be autonomic?

1 non-prescription drugs
2 garden plants
3 vacations
4 outside entertainment
5 child's clothing

A 1 and 2
B 1 and 3
C 2 and 3
D 3 and 4
E 4 and 5

3.43*

A subway advertisement in New York City depicted a Chinese man biting into a sandwich and was captioned, 'You don't have to be Jewish to love Levy's Real Jewish Rye Bread'. The advertisement suggests the actions of which processes?

1 ethnocentricity
2 de-ethnicitization
3 acculturation
4 cultural interpenetration
5 assimilation

A 1 and 2
B 1 and 3
C 2 and 3
D 3 and 4
E 4 and 5

3.44

An American study indicated that average black household income in 1984 was only 63 per cent of white, but that both blacks and whites spent about two-thirds of their incomes on housing, transportation, and food. From this, it is possible to conclude that:

A black purchasing behaviour may depend more on income level than on race or culture

B blacks are more likely than whites to have higher occupational aspirations

C black purchasing behaviour has been disproportionately influenced by black concentration in central cities

D blacks are more likely than whites to hold materialistic views

E middle- and higher-income black groups are better markets to target than lower-income black groups

3.45

Which of the following is **invalid** as a criterion for dividing a society into social classes?

A there must be clear boundaries between the classes

B the classes must have a vertical order to them, defining their status

C an individual can belong to only one social class

D there must be behavioural variations between the classes

E behaviours associated with one particular social class cannot be shared with other social classes

3.46*

The best objective single proxy indicator of social-class standing is:

A income

B postal address

C occupation

D possessions

E level of education

3.47

Which criticism is **invalid** in relation to the use of social class as a segmentation variable?

A the class with which consumers identify may differ from the one to which they objectively belong

B a person may be assigned to a social class without meeting all the relevant criteria

C rankings of occupational status tend to be unstable over time

D the automatic equation of a wife's social status with that of her husband is no longer appropriate

E consumers' aspirations of upward social mobility have distorted certain behavioural patterns

3.48*

In the analysis of consumer behaviour:

A the differences between subcultures, and the differences between social classes, are both major

B the differences between subcultures are major, and the differences between social classes are minor

C the differences between subcultures are minor, and the differences between social classes are major

D the differences between subcultures, and the differences between social classes, are both minor

E the differences between subcultures, and the differences between social classes, cannot be compared

3.49

Which of the following variables is **not** normally associated with family life-cycle (FLC) analysis?

A marital status

B size of family

C age of family members

D occupation of head of household

E interests of family members

3.50

A 'dust off your dancing shoes' theme for a holiday cruise advertisement would seem to be targeted at which FLC group?

A young singles

B newly married couples

C full nesters

D empty nesters

E solitary survivors

INDUSTRIAL AND ORGANIZATIONAL MARKETING

4.1

Which of the following is **not** part of the industrial market?

A agriculture

B communications

C hotels

D merchants

E banking

4.2

Which of the following statements **incorrectly** compares the buying process in industrial and consumer marketing?

A industrial buying is frequently a group-decision process, whereas consumer buying can be individual or group

B post-purchase evaluation is likely to be less important in industrial buying than in consumer buying

C there is greater interdependence between buyer and seller in industrial buying than in consumer buying

D personal selling is more important in industrial marketing than consumer marketing

E price negotiation is more likely in industrial marketing than in consumer marketing

4.3*

Which of the following statements **inaccurately** differentiates between organizational and consumer markets?

A organizational markets are more difficult to segment than consumer markets

B the demand of organizational consumers is more subject to cyclical fluctuations than is consumer demand

C organizational consumers are fewer in number and more geographically concentrated than are final consumers

D the distribution channel for organizational consumers is normally shorter than for final consumers

E industrial buying is based on derived demand, whereas consumer buying represents direct demand

4.4

A glass manufacturer advertising to persuade consumers to buy drinks in glass bottles is attempting to:

A support personal selling

B stimulate direct demand

C stimulate derived demand

D support brand advertising

E none of these

4.5

Which of the following **cannot** be considered an industrial product?

A component parts

B major equipment

C industrial services

D consumable supplies

E none of these

4.6

If the price of shirt buttons increases by 20 per cent, we can expect short-term demand for shirt buttons to:

A increase slightly

B increase substantially

C remain about the same

D decrease slightly

E decrease substantially

4.7*
A straight rebuy would involve which of these stages in the industrial buying process?

1 problem recognition
2 order-routine specification
3 proposal solicitation
4 product specification
5 performance review

A 1 and 2
B 1 and 3
C 2 and 3
D 3 and 4
E 4 and 5

4.8*
Which of the following statements **incorrectly** compares straight rebuys with modified rebuys?

A re-ordering is on a routine basis in a straight rebuy, but requires reconsideration of some aspect in a modified rebuy

B the purchasing department chooses only one supplier in a straight rebuy, but may choose two or more in a modified rebuy

C 'out-suppliers' typically try to get a 'foot-in-the-door' trial order from companies in straight rebuy situations, but frequently choose the 'better offer' approach in modified rebuy situations

D straight rebuys are characterized by habit, whereas modified rebuys are characterized by complex decision-making

E straight rebuys are more likely for low-priced, frequently purchased products, whereas modified rebuys are more likely for higher-priced, less frequently purchased products

4.9
The Exquisite Form ladies' underwear company in the UK operates a programme whereby a retailer's stock levels of Exquisite Form products are mutually agreed, and an Exquisite Form representative visits each retail location on a regular basis to take an inventory, re-order stock, and replace slower-selling lines with new or faster-selling lines. Exquisite Form's intention(s) seem(s) to be to:

A encourage straight rebuys
B encourage modified rebuys
C encourage new-task purchasing

D A and B
E B and C

4.10
Which of the following statements **incorrectly** distinguishes new-task buying situations from modified rebuy situations?

A new-task buying situations are generally more complex

B new-task buying situations generally require more time to decision completion

C new-task buying situations require a more varied communications mix

D new-task buying situations often involve greater risk

E new-task buying situations are less likely to be affected by intrapersonal influences

4.11
Salespeople usually have their greatest impact at which stage of new-task buying?

A awareness
B trial
C evaluation
D adoption
E interest

4.12
People who have the power to determine what information or which sellers can reach the buying centre are called:

A influencers
B approvers
C initiators
D deciders
E gatekeepers

4.13*
Which of the following statements **incorrectly** compares industrial with consumer market demand forecasting?

A there are usually fewer industrial buyers than final consumers

B the cost of carrying out an intention survey relating to industrial buyers is normally lower than one for final consumers

C a problem in forecasting either industrial or consumer demand is determining how firm the
   expressed purchasing intentions are

D industrial buyers have clearer intentions than final
   consumers

E none of these

4.14*

Which of the following constitute organizational influences on the industrial buying process?

1 the buying centre's preferences
2 the buyer's attitude towards risk
3 practices of vendor evaluation
4 the corporate culture
5 rate of technological change

A 1 and 2
B 1 and 3
C 2 and 3
D 3 and 4
E 4 and 5

Case Study 4.1:
Purchasing screening membranes

A multinational chemicals manufacturer based in
Britain has had a problem achieving certain anti-pol-
lution standards for water discharged from its factories. Knowing this, a small British company producing
screening membranes has sent a sample to the chemicals manufacturer, and this has now been sent to the
manufacturer's research laboratories for testing. The
engineer doing the tests is convinced that the screening membrane meets all requirements, but is reluctant
to recommend it because, he says, he has never heard
of the company and does not want to risk his job on an
'unknown quantity'.

Questions 4.15–4.17 relate to this case study

4.15

The engineer's role in the buying process would normally be that of:

A buyer
B decider
C influencer
D approver
E gatekeeper

4.16*

In the event, the buying process has become dysfunc-
tional because:

1 the engineer has let personal factors override professional judgement
2 the required specifications for the product have been
   inadequately defined
3 the chemicals manufacturer's organizational policies have made decision-making too complex
4 the engineer has not kept to his assigned role in the
   decision process
5 the membrane manufacturer apparently suffers from
   marketing myopia

A 1 and 2
B 1 and 3
C 2 and 3
D 3 and 4
E 4 and 5

4.17*

Assuming that no decision has yet been announced, the
most promising course of action for the membrane manufacturer would be to:

A advertise in the trade press to build up the company's reputation

B advertise the company's product in the trade press

C send a sales team to the chemicals manufacturer

D offer a significant discount in return for an immediate order

E send a technical team to the chemicals manufacturer

4.18

Which of the following statements **incorrectly** compares market segmentation for industrial goods with
that for consumer goods?

A it is easier to identify organizational needs than individual needs

B industrial segmentation is likely to be more specific than consumer segmentation

C industrial segmentation is more likely to lead to
   implications for personal selling

D segmentation is used less frequently in industrial
   markets than in consumer markets

E segmentation criteria are the same for both markets, but the descriptors are different

4.19*

A components manufacturer is best advised to adopt which segmentation strategy?

A undifferentiated

B concentrated

C differentiated

D customized

E cannot be determined

4.20*

The descriptor of 'performance requirements' in industrial marketing segmentation is analogous to which of the following descriptors in consumer marketing segmentation?

A brand preference

B size of purchase

C proneness to make a deal

D user status

E quality

4.21

The descriptor of 'corporate culture' in industrial marketing segmentation is analogous to which of the following descriptors in consumer marketing segmentation?

A life-cycle stage

B income

C family size

D age, gender, race

E lifestyle

4.22

The descriptor of 'type of industry' in industrial marketing segmentation is analogous to which of the following descriptors in consumer marketing segmentation?

A life-cycle stage

B income

C family size

D age, gender, race

E lifestyle

4.23

In relation to industrial marketing, which of the following are demographic segmentation variables?

1 technology

2 customer service requirements

3 industry

4 customer size

5 user status

A 1 and 2

B 1 and 3

C 2 and 3

D 3 and 4

E 4 and 5

4.24

If a manufacturer decides to concentrate on companies with which it has a strong existing relationship, it is using which category of industrial segmentation variables?

A purchasing approaches

B situational factors

C personal characteristics

D operating variables

E benefits sought

4.25*

A study found that advertising was a relatively unimportant influence on industrial buyers. This reflects the fact that:

A industrial advertising is designed not so much to influence purchases as to create product and company awareness

B industrial buyers are motivated solely by economic factors

C trade publications lack credibility among industrial buyers

D the industrial advertising budget of most companies is too small

E the frequent employment of long texts in industrial advertising seriously reduces its impact

4.26

If a manufacturer decides to concentrate on certain, rather than all, applications of its product, it is using which category of industrial segmentation variables?

A purchasing approaches

B situational factors

C personal characteristics

D operating variables

E benefits sought

4.27

Complete market segmentation might be a good market strategy for manufacturers of:

1 airframes for aircraft

2 ships

3 trucks

4 televisions

5 railway engines

A 1 and 2

B 1 and 3

C 2 and 3

D 3 and 4

E 4 and 5

4.28

For a non-differentiated industrial product such as cement, which element(s) of the marketing mix usually receive(s) most emphasis?

A channels of distribution

B promotion

C price

D A and B

E B and C

4.29

Which of the following **incorrectly** compares industrial and consumer marketing in terms of products?

A products tend to be more complex for industrial markets than for consumer markets

B product specifications are usually more important for industrial markets than for consumer markets

C technological development is likely to be more important for industrial products than for consumer products

D the value of the order is usually higher for industrial consumers than for final consumers

E application of the marketing concept is further advanced in marketing industrial products than in marketing consumer products

4.30

Which of the following is **unlikely** to be found as part of the services/product dimension of an industrial marketing mix?

A guaranteed delivery schedules

B quality control

C custom design

D research and development

E manufacturer-sponsored advertising

4.31*

Compared with consumer marketing mixes, the product ingredients of industrial marketing mixes often include a greater emphasis on:

A services

B packaging

C brand name

D features

E quality

4.32

Which of the following are useful in discouraging small orders to manufacturers?

1 non-cumulative quantity discounts

2 cumulative quantity discounts

3 minimum order sizes

4 discounts for prompt payment

5 establishing a network of distributors

A 1 and 2

B 1 and 3

C 2 and 3

D 3 and 4

E 4 and 5

4.33

When a dress buyer for a department store chain is putting a garment through product-value analysis, which of the following questions is **least** likely to be considered?

A can a cheaper material be used for the collar lining?

B is this vendor reliable?

C can the hem be reduced by one inch?

D will another dependable supplier provide a similar garment for less?

E will the garment's cost allow the chain to make a sufficiently large mark-up?

4.34

Which price determination methods are most common in industrial markets?

1 marginal revenue pricing
2 perceived value pricing
3 target return pricing
4 cost-plus pricing
5 break-even analysis

A 1 and 2
B 1 and 3
C 2 and 3
D 3 and 4
E 4 and 5

4.35*

Which of the following statements **fails** to explain why price is more important as a determinant of sales in industrial marketing than in consumer marketing?

A industrial buyers are more likely to use cost criteria in evaluating alternative products
B prices set by different suppliers are likely to show much more variation because of differences in specifications and terms of sale
C negotiated prices are more likely in industrial sales
D derived demand tends to be more subject to cyclical swings than final demand
E tendered bids are frequently requested in industrial marketing

4.36

Which of the following is usually **not** a policy objective of industrial pricing?

A to avoid customer and political criticism
B to discourage competitors from entering the market
C to maximize short-term profits
D to penetrate the market
E to avoid unduly provocative competitive action

4.37*

Which of the following sequences depicts the relative importance usually attached to various promotional tools by industrial goods companies (most important factor listed first)?

A personal selling, advertising, sales promotion, public relations
B sales promotion, public relations, personal selling, advertising
C advertising, personal selling, sales promotion, public relations
D personal selling, sales promotion, advertising, public relations
E public relations, personal selling, advertising, sales promotion

4.38*

Total marketing expenditure as a percentage of sales (the M/S ratio) would be expected to fall:

1 as the product life cycle progresses
2 as the customer growth rate increases
3 as market share increases
4 as the amount spent on advertising as a percentage of the marketing budget (the A/M ratio) falls
5 as sales fall

A 1 and 2
B 1 and 3
C 2 and 3
D 3 and 4
E 4 and 5

4.39*

Which of the following statements reflects the typical relationship between sales volume and the allocation of advertising budgets to various media?

A the higher the sales volume, the more the use of trade shows, industrial films, and trade, technical, and house publications, and the less the use of sales promotion and direct mail
B the higher the sales volume, the more the use of direct mail and trade, technical, and house publications, and the less the use of sales promotion, trade shows, and industrial films
C the higher the sales volume, the more the use of sales promotion and direct mail, and the less the use of trade shows, industrial films, and trade, technical, and house publications
D the higher the sales volume, the more the use of sales promotion, trade shows, and industrial films, and the less the use of direct mail and trade, technical, and house publications
E the higher the sales volume, the less the use of trade shows, industrial films, sales promotion, direct mail, and trade, technical, and house publications

4.40*

In terms of promotional budget, a little-known, small company with limited funds is best advised to:

A concentrate on building up the company's reputation in advertisements

B concentrate on selecting and training good sales representatives

C concentrate on advertising the company's products

D put equal emphasis on sales representatives and product advertising

E put equal emphasis on product advertising and reputation advertising

4.41*

In terms of promotional budget, a well-known, large company is best advised to:

A concentrate on building up the company's reputation in advertisements

B concentrate on selecting and training good sales representatives

C concentrate on advertising the company's products

D put equal emphasis on sales representatives and product advertising

E put equal emphasis on product advertising and reputation advertising

4.42

Which of the following statements **incorrectly** contrasts business-to-business industrial advertising with consumer advertising?

A business-to-business advertising tends to be technical and factual in content, whereas consumer advertising tends to emphasize brand image

B business-to-business advertising seldom results in immediate, measurable sales, unlike consumer advertising

C the product usage cycle is long with business-to-business advertising, but relatively short for most items with consumer advertising

D business-to-business advertising is a major sales influence, whereas consumer advertising generally supports the sales influence

E business-to-business advertising tends to pinpoint only a very few publications for use, whereas consumer advertising tends to favour a balanced schedule of several publications

4.43

Which of the following is **not** a typical function of industrial advertising?

A furthering a pull strategy

B building understanding of new products and features in the minds of prospects

C efficient reminding in anticipation of a change in buyer readiness stage

D lead generation

E reassurance of prospects about their purchase

4.44

Industrial goods channel systems differ from consumer goods channel systems in that the former:

1 are more likely to offer exclusive territories to their distributors

2 are more likely to use push than pull strategies

3 are usually longer

4 are less selective in coverage

5 depend less on control over physical distribution activities

A 1 and 2

B 1 and 3

C 2 and 3

D 3 and 4

E 4 and 5

4.45

When an industrial goods manufacturer uses its company sales force to sell directly to industrial manufacturers, this is an example of a:

A zero-level channel

B one-level channel

C two-level channel

D three-level channel

E backward channel

4.46

When an industrial goods manufacturer uses manufacturer's representatives to sell to industrial distributors who sell to industrial customers, this is an example of a:

A zero-level channel

B one-level channel

C two-level channel

D three-level channel

E backward channel

4.47

When an industrial goods manufacturer uses its company sales force to sell to industrial distributors who sell to industrial customers, this is an example of a:

A zero-level channel

B one-level channel

C two-level channel

D three-level channel

E backward channel

4.48

Which of the following is **not** a disadvantage encountered when using an industrial distributor?

A industrial distributors may lack the technical knowledge necessary to sell and service certain industrial items

B industrial distributors frequently stock competing brands

C industrial distributors are less likely to handle bulky items and slow sellers

D the producer's capital requirements are increased in order to provide the distributor's inventories

E being independent, industrial distributors are difficult for producers to control

4.49*

A sales agent is generally superior to a company direct sales force when:

1 the manufacturer produces a narrow line of products

2 the manufacturer wants to employ a push strategy

3 the sales volume is relatively small

4 the manufacturer wants to reach all members of a given trade group

5 the manufacturer wants to dispose of the entire output through a single intermediary

A 1 and 2

B 1 and 3

C 2 and 3

D 3 and 4

E 4 and 5

4.50*

A manufacturer's agent is generally superior to a company direct sales force when:

1 the manufacturer produces a narrow line of products

2 the manufacturer wants to employ a push strategy

3 the sales volume is relatively small

4 the manufacturer wants to reach all members of a given trade group

5 the manufacturer wants to dispose of the entire output through a single intermediary

A 1 and 2

B 1 and 3

C 2 and 3

D 3 and 4

E 4 and 5

5

COMPETITIVE MARKETING STRATEGY

5.1*
A company deciding to focus more attention on the fast-growing quality-sensitive segment and avoid cutting prices, even though the deal-prone customer segment is also growing, is displaying a:

A market orientation

B product orientation

C competition orientation

D price orientation

E customer orientation

5.2
A company deciding to leave a market because it cannot afford to fight the competition is displaying a:

A market orientation

B product orientation

C competition orientation

D price orientation

E customer orientation

5.3
A company which undertakes competitive analysis before deciding whether to target a particular market segment is displaying a:

A market orientation

B product orientation

C competition orientation

D price orientation

E customer orientation

5.4*
In a given city, a number of hosiery shops and a number of department stores are selling similar hosiery products. This is an example of:

A generic competition

B product market competition

C free-form competition

D inter-type competition

E market segment competition

5.5*
Manufacturers of conventional film cameras are concerned about the introduction of electronic imaging cameras. This is an example of:

A generic competition

B product market competition

C free-form competition

D inter-type competition

E market segment competition

5.6*
A number of multi-screen cinema complexes in the same city are showing three of the same films. This is an example of:

A generic competition

B product market competition

C free-form competition

D inter-type competition

E market segment competition

5.7*
A car manufacturer sees itself as competing with companies that sell major consumer durables, foreign vacations, new homes, etc. This company is aware of:

A generic competition

B product market competition

C free-form competition

D inter-type competition

E market segment competition

5.8

The notion of a competitive advantage in a product market centres on a firm providing:

A a unique product or service

B the greatest product range among competitors

C the lowest price among competitors

D a unique customer benefit

E market-share leadership

5.9*

Which of the following are **not** advantages of being first in a product-market?

1 the greatest opportunity to dominate the market

2 reduced risk

3 best terms from suppliers

4 cost reductions due to learning curve effects

5 enhanced reputation

A 1 and 2

B 1 and 3

C 2 and 3

D 3 and 4

E 4 and 5

5.10

A company entering a product market relatively early after the first firm is likely to find that:

1 successful entry will require less marketing effort than if the company had been first

2 customers are more likely to be switchers from the first company than to be new prospects

3 early entry can reduce waste in resources

4 most of the market opportunity still exists

5 the first firm's reaction will be muted because of its preoccupation with its own product launch

A 1 and 2

B 1 and 3

C 2 and 3

D 3 and 4

E 4 and 5

5.11*

A company entering an already established product market containing a number of competitors is best advised to:

1 target the largest market segment

2 spend more than incumbent firms on sales force, advertising, and promotion

3 offer a specialist product line

4 claim that product quality is superior to incumbent firms

5 create a new channel of distribution

A 1 and 2

B 1 and 3

C 2 and 3

D 3 and 4

E 4 and 5

5.12

In general, prices among competitors will tend to be very similar, if not identical, in:

1 pure monopoly

2 pure competition

3 pure oligopoly

4 differentiated oligopoly

5 monopolistic competition

A 1 and 2

B 1 and 3

C 2 and 3

D 3 and 4

E 4 and 5

5.13*

Price wars are most likely in markets where:

1 a number of significant factors differentiate among competitors

2 cost differentiation among competitors is crucial to setting prices

3 competitors are nearly identical

4 there are a lot of competitors

5 one firm has a commanding market-share advantage over its competitors

A 1 and 2

B 1 and 3

C 2 and 3

D 3 and 4

E 4 and 5

5.14

According to Porter's generic strategy model, a firm with a low market share can succeed more easily by adopting a:

A cost leadership strategy

B focus strategy

C differentiation strategy

D A or B

E B or C

5.15*

According to Porter's generic strategy model, a cost leadership strategy differs from a focus strategy in that the former:

A offers more distinctive products

B appeals to a broader market

C offers lower prices

D has better profit margins

E offers fewer products

5.16*

The strategic importance of a company increasing its relative market share in its served market is that:

A market share is a good indicator of managerial competence and product quality

B profits and return on investment tend to rise as a company's market share rises

C small competitors cannot reap the same economies of scale

D high market-share companies attract better staff than those with low market share

E a company with low market share is liable to be forced out of business

5.17*

Which of the following phenomena are characteristic of companies showing market-share gains?

1 they typically develop and add more new products to their line

2 they cut prices more deeply than competitors

3 they pay more attention to reducing overheads than do competitors

4 they increase their product quality relative to competitors

5 they increase their marketing expenditure faster than the rate of market growth

A 1 and 2

B 1 and 3

C 2 and 3

D 3 and 4

E 4 and 5

5.18*

The use of market share to judge a company's performance relative to the competition may be criticized on all but which of the following grounds?

A it is not possible to isolate the factor(s) responsible for change in market share

B a decline in market share may not indicate that the company is performing any worse than other competitors

C market-share decline could indicate an attempt to increase profits

D not all shifts in market share have marketing significance

E it is not always valid to judge a company's performance against the average performance of all companies

5.19

If a car model is said to have 28 per cent market share of cars in its class, we can conclude that:

A the company's overall market share will be less than 28 per cent

B the company's overall market share will equal 28 per cent

C the company's overall market share will exceed 28 per cent

D there is insufficient information to estimate the size of the company's overall market share

E the terminology is inappropriate for market-share analysis, and thus the statement is meaningless

5.20

A market-share gain strategy is normally **inadvisable** for a company when:

A it has suffered significant share losses through competitors' actions

B it has a very great lead over its competitors

C the competition has shown vulnerability

D return on investment is below reasonable expectations

E a recent acquisition permits the potential for increased share

5.21

The strategy to seek to maintain a market-share *status quo* is most suitable when:

A the market is volatile and unstable

B new products are being launched in the market

C the market is inadequately served by competition

D market profitability is declining

E competitors are attempting to enter the market or to expand their market share

5.22

The harvesting strategy of extracting maximum benefit from the market share while preparing to exit the market is most suitable when:

A the market is volatile and unstable

B new products are being launched in the market

C the market is inadequately served by competition

D market profitability is declining

E competitors are attempting to enter the market or to expand their market share

5.23

The strategy of attempting to reduce risk associated with high market share without reducing this share is most suitable when:

A the market is volatile and unstable

B new products are being launched in the market

C the market is inadequately served by competition

D market profitability is declining

E competitors are attempting to enter the market or to expand their market share

5.24

In an emerging industry, especially one affected by new technology and changing needs of buyers, the most promising competitive position for a market leader would be to seek:

A differential advantage

B market domination

C market withdrawal

D product/market selectivity

E market development

5.25*

Which of the following characteristics would tend to be detrimental to the success of a low-share business?

A frequent purchase of products and supplies

B standardized products with few extra services

C high-growth markets

D industries in which products have high added value

E markets for industrial components or supplies

5.26

In a declining market, the most promising competitive position for a market challenger would be to seek:

A differential advantage

B market domination

C market withdrawal

D product/market selectivity

E market development

5.27

In a declining market, the most promising competitive position for a market follower would be to seek:

A differential advantage

B market domination

C market withdrawal

D product/market selectivity

E market development

5.28

In a fragmented industry characterized by a large number of relatively small firms, the most promising competitive position for a market nicher would be to seek:

A differential advantage

B market domination

C market withdrawal

D product/market selectivity

E market development

5.29

Some ladies' fashion houses have introduced exclusive brands and also mass market brands to complement their couture designs. This is an example of which market defence strategy?

A pre-emptive defence

B mobile defence

C flanking defence

D position defence

E counter-offensive

5.30

A new liquid detergent, Radion, was launched by Lever Brothers in Britain in 1990 with the promise that it would remove 'stale odours'. Almost simultaneously, Procter & Gamble ran a television campaign for its well-established liquid detergent, Ariel, with a housewife saying she was not bothered about stale odours because she used Ariel. Procter & Gamble appears to be pursuing which defence strategy?

A pre-emptive defence

B mobile defence

C flanking defence

D position defence

E counter-offensive

5.31

Market broadening and market diversification are linked with which defence strategy?

A pre-emptive defence

B mobile defence

C flanking defence

D position defence

E counter-offensive

5.32*

Competitive rivalry is likely to be the most intense in industries characterized by:

1 high inventory costs

2 capital intensiveness

3 stagnant primary demand

4 production of standardized items

5 high fixed costs

A 1 and 2

B 1 and 3

C 2 and 3

D 3 and 4

E 4 and 5

5.33*

Which of the following characteristics does **not** necessarily typify a market leader in a product market?

A it usually leads other firms in price changes

B its products are usually of higher quality than other firms

C it is usually first with new-product introductions

D it usually has the largest distribution coverage

E it usually has the highest promotional intensity

5.34*

The likelihood of an attack on a market leader is increased when:

1 the market exhibits a high growth rate

2 the leader has followed a price-skimming policy

3 substitute technology emerges in the industry

4 the leader cuts its advertising expenditure

5 the leader is relatively small compared with other firms in the market

A 1 and 2

B 1 and 3

C 2 and 3

D 3 and 4

E 4 and 5

5.35*

A market leader whose policy it is to develop new-product ideas, improve customer services, increase staff productivity, and cut costs is attempting to:

A expand the market

B implement a position defence

C defend market share

D implement a pre-emptive defence

E implement a reactive defence

5.36

Television advertisements for Sainsbury's supermarkets, the UK market leader, show how to make interesting recipes using ingredients from Sainsbury's. This is an example of:

A developing new uses for the products

B developing more usage of the products

C developing a new group of users

D developing market signals to dissuade competitors from attacking

E developing product differentiation

5.37

An important difference between a market challenger and a market follower is that:

A challengers hold a bigger market share than followers

B challengers attack the market leader, whereas followers do not

C challengers receive greater returns on investment than followers

D challengers have higher profit margins than followers

E challengers follow a policy of market growth, whereas followers do not

5.38*

Which of the following market challenger strategies carries the greatest risk to the challenger?

A attacking a firm its own size

B attacking the market leader

C attacking a smaller firm

D introducing flanker brands

E changing channels of distribution

5.39

In an advertisement stating that a majority of men believe that Bic's single-edged razor shaves closer than Gillette's double-edged Trac II, Bic asked rhetorically, 'Why pay the difference when there's no difference?' This is an example of:

A a flank attack

B a bypass attack

C a guerrilla attack

D a frontal attack

E an encirclement attack

5.40

In the American ketchup battle of the early 1960s, Hunts attacked the market leader, Heinz, by introducing two new flavours, undercutting Heinz on price, offering heavy trade allowances to retailers, and raising the advertising budget to twice the Heinz level. This is an example of:

A a flank attack

B a bypass attack

C a guerrilla attack

D a frontal attack

E an encirclement attack

5.41

An advertisement appeared in a free newspaper circulated in several small towns in north Nottinghamshire: 'Bumps & Boobs, Retford's leading ladies' underwear shop ... and we're just down the road in Worksop.' This is an example of:

A a flank attack

B a bypass attack

C a guerrilla attack

D a frontal attack

E an encirclement attack

5.42*

A market follower is **unlikely** to adopt which of the strategies below?

1 attempt to obtain a competitive advantage in distribution

2 engage in intensive advertising

3 introduce carbon copies of leading brands

4 follow the leader in pricing

5 try to keep manufacturing costs low and product quality high

A 1 and 2

B 1 and 3

C 2 and 3

D 3 and 4

E 4 and 5

5.43

A follower who maintains some differentiation from a leader but follows in such things as innovations, general price levels, and distribution is:

A a close follower

B a cloner follower

C a selective follower

D a distant follower

E an adapter follower

5.44*

A follower is most likely to provoke retaliation if it adopts which of these policies?

A entry into a new market as it opens up

B specialized credit facilities

C location specialization

D service specialization

E substantial product innovation

5.45*

Which of the following comparisons between market nichers and mass marketers is correct?

A the nicher aims for high margin, whereas the mass marketer aims for high volume

B the tendency is for nichers to move towards mass marketing, and for mass marketers to move towards niche marketing

C nichers attract less competition than mass marketers

D niching is appropriate only for small firms, and mass marketing only for large firms

E market niching tends to be riskier than mass marketing

5.46

An ideal niche would **not necessarily** have which of the following characteristics?

A growth potential

B geographical concentration of customers

C negligible interest to major competitors

D strong relationship between the firm and its customers

E easy customer accessibility

5.47

Which of the following is **not** usually associated with a market niche strategy?

A serving a specialist market

B price competition

C serving a limited geographical area

D appealing to a specific segment of the market

E focusing on a narrow product line

5.48

Which of the following roles is **inappropriate** for a market nicher?

A vertical-level specialist

B customer-size specialist

C specific-customer specialist

D market specialist

E product-line specialist

5.49

A real-estate agent who specialized in selling only country cottages is engaged in which niche?

A end-user

B quality/price

C product feature

D service

E channel

5.50

The Patek Philippe company of Geneva claims that its watches are the finest in the world, made with a total disregard of how long it takes to bring 'absolute perfection'. Patek Philippe is engaged in which niche?

A end-user

B quality/price

C product feature

D service

E channel

6

PRODUCTS AND PRODUCT CONCEPTS

6.1
A consumer is unsure whether to buy a mouthwash, a toothpaste, an antiseptic gargle, or a package of strong mints, suggesting:

A the consumer is seeking intangible benefits rather than a specific product

B the consumer is seeking tangible benefits rather than a specific product

C the consumer is considering augmented products rather than the tangible (or core) product

D the products being considered lack strong brand identity

E the customer is seeking a single product which combines multiple product features

6.2*
Which of the following products is the odd one out?

A a loaf of white bread

B a caffeine-free diet cola

C a ten-gear lightweight racing bicycle

D a King's pattern stainless steel set of cutlery

E a low freezing-point diesel fuel

6.3*
The preferred marketing mix strategy for shopping goods is to:

A emphasize low price

B gain widespread distribution at low cost

C gain adequate representation in major shopping districts or large shopping centres

D promote the product through aggressive personal selling

E distribute the product through a limited number of outlets

6.4*
The preferred marketing mix strategy for specialty goods is to:

A emphasize low price

B gain widespread distribution at low cost

C gain adequate representation in major shopping districts or large shopping centres

D promote the product through aggressive personal selling

E distribute the product through a limited number of outlets

6.5
Which of the following could **not** be defined as a product line?

A pan shiners, furniture polish, window cleaning spray

B frankfurters, sausages, hamburgers

C hair colouring, hair spray, shampoo

D a mid-market range of goods sold under a single brand

E all of the above may be defined as product lines

6.6*
In formulating marketing strategy, which of the following **cannot** be considered an important advantage of grouping products into a product line?

A a product line reduces the chance of cannibalizing sales from other company products

B product lines provide economies of scale in advertising

C product lines provide an opportunity to standardize components

D a product line allows for package uniformity

E a product line allows the company to follow a policy of price lining

6.7

Which of the following is **not** an advantage if a firm operates a full-line strategy?

A more items carried should produce more chances to make a sale

B the company may benefit over competitors due to economies of scale in production

C despatching more items from one source may lower total transportation cost

D a full line may permit co-ordination of product offerings

E customers may prefer to deal with one supplier to simplify their buying

6.8

Which of the following is **not** an advantage if a firm operates a limited-line strategy?

A buyers may prefer limited-line suppliers in the belief that savings through specialization are passed on to them

B consumer recognition of a brand is usually higher for limited-line producers than for full-line producers

C a limited product offering may be more closely related to specific targets or segments

D buyers may prefer limited-line suppliers as a more certain source of supply

E the line can be limited to include only high-profit items

6.9

Product-line mapping refers to:

A the percentage of total sales contributed by each item in the line

B the percentage of total profits contributed by each item in the line

C determining the ideal product for a particular market segment

D how the product line is positioned against competitors' product lines

E none of these

6.10*

Which of the following statements is **incorrect** in relation to determining the optimal length of a product line?

A companies that emphasize high profitability tend to carry shorter lines

B a product line is too long if profits can be increased by dropping items

C companies seeking high market share and market growth tend to carry longer lines irrespective of whether all the items contribute to profits

D a product line is at its optimal length when additions or deletions do not affect the profitability of other products in the line

E a product line is too short if profits can be increased by adding items

6.11

Which of the following represent **inadvisable** attempts at line filling?

1 a company selling silk ties adds a new range of polyester ties

2 a firm selling shirts at £16.95, £21.95, and £26.95 introduces a new range at £17.95

3 a manufacturer producing low-end and high-end pianos decides to complete its range with mid-market pianos

4 a mid-market manufacturer introduces a new high-quality calculator to sell at a lower price than a similar one from the market leader

5 a retailer selling skirts composed of 75 per cent polyester and 25 per cent cotton adds a range composed of 25 per cent polyester and 75 per cent cotton

A 1 and 2

B 1 and 3

C 2 and 3

D 3 and 4

E 4 and 5

6.12*

A firm seeking to add new offerings to a line to appeal to an existing market is engaging in which product-line strategy?

A line holding

B line expansion

C line retrenchment

D line extension

E line repositioning

6.13*

A firm seeking to add new offerings to a line to appeal to a new market is engaging in which product-line strategy?

A line holding

B line expansion

C line retrenchment

D line extension

E line repositioning

6.14*

When Scott Paper found its sales of relatively high-priced, high-quality toilet tissues and paper towels decreasing in the late 1970s, it decided to reduce the price of its existing line by changing the paper composition, and at the same time to promote the lower-price line heavily. Scott Paper was following which product-line strategy?

A line holding

B line expansion

C line retrenchment

D line extension

E line repositioning

6.15*

A downward stretch of a product line would be **inadvisable** for a company if:

A the new item is likely to cannibalize items at a time when competition is sharp at the high end

B the new product has a different brand quality image

C slower growth is taking place at the high end

D the decision is in response to an attack against it at the high end

E there is a market hole, but no obvious competitor, at the low end

6.16

Which of the following statements comparing upward with two-way stretches is **untrue**?

A customer up-trading is more likely for an upward stretch company than for a two-way stretch company

B a company following either strategy is trying to position itself as a full-line firm

C two-way stretches usually require more resources than upward stretches

D an upward stretch is likely to be completed more quickly than a two-way stretch

E none of these

6.17

In a product mix, the difference between product-mix breadth and product-mix length is that:

A product-mix breadth refers to how many different product lines the company carries, whereas product-mix length refers to how many variants are offered of each product in the line

B product-mix breadth refers to how many variants are offered of each product in the line, whereas product-mix length refers to how many different items are in the mix

C product-mix breadth refers to how many different items are in the mix, whereas product-mix length refers to how many different product lines the company carries

D product-mix breadth refers to how many different product lines the company carries, whereas product-mix length refers to how many different items are in the mix

E product-mix breadth refers to how many different items are in the mix, whereas product-mix length refers to how many variants are offered of each product in the line

6.18

Sales of French champagne declined from 249 million bottles in 1989 to 214 million in 1992. Aggressive pricing during the high demand period of the 1980s (nearly doubling the price in the decade) and the slowdown in the world economy have been blamed partly for the decline. Meanwhile, consumption of lower priced champagne-type wines from Australia, the United States, and Spain has increased. From this, we can conclude that:

1 customers are showing increased price sensitivity for champagne

2 product substitution is operating

3 the quality of French champagne is declining

4 the price-quality relationship is no longer important for French champagne

5 the quality of non-French champagne is improving

A 1 and 2

B 1 and 3

C 2 and 3

D 3 and 4

E 4 and 5

6.19*

Companies owned by General Mills include Betty Crocker (cake mixes), Yoplait (yogurts), York Steak Houses and Red Lobster Inns (restaurants), Parker Brothers (games), Lionel Trains (scale trains), and Izod/Lacoste (clothing). Its product-mix can be said to show:

1 relatively wide breadth

2 relatively low consistency

3 relatively short length

4 relatively deep depth

5 relative emphasis on external acquisition versus internal development

A 1 and 2

B 1 and 3

C 2 and 3

D 3 and 4

E 4 and 5

6.20

Which of the following is **not** a product-differentiation variable?

A delivery

B features

C performance

D durability

E style

Table 6.1
Comparison of company costs and perceived value for product features

Feature	Company cost (£)	Consumer perceived value (£)
Slow reverse	5	5
Extra (third) recording head	22	65
Improved remote control	10	30
Tape wear warning light	5	10

6.21

Suppose that a producer of a video recorder (VCR) could add only one of four new features to a model. Each feature would cost a certain amount, and market research indicates that consumers place differing values on each feature, as indicated in Table 6.1. The feature that should be added is:

A slow reverse

B extra (third) recording head

C improved remote control

D tape wear warning light

E cannot be determined from the information provided

6.22

If the company now finds it is able to cut its costs for an extra (third) recording head to £16, which feature should be added?

A slow reverse

B extra (third) recording head

C improved remote control

D tape wear warning light

E cannot be determined from the information provided

Case Study 6.1
Miele automatic washing machines

Miele automatic washing machines, which sell at the top end of the market in Britain, come with a one-year guarantee on parts and labour. Purchasers are offered a Double Cover warranty on parts (excluding labour) for a further four years for an additional payment of £7.50. Similar extended warranties for competing brands usually cost £30-50 for a further two or three years.

Questions 6.23–6.25 relate to this case study

6.23

The pricing of the Miele extended warranty suggests that:

A the machine is inexpensive to repair

B the manufacturers are convinced of the machine's reliability

C customers would not pay more, given the high initial purchase price

D repair costs for years 2–5 are built into the selling price

E the Miele warranty is inferior to that of competitors

6.24

In demonstrating the Miele machine, the salesperson says that it does not have to be bolted or screwed to the floor, but yet will fast-spin clothes with so little vibration that a cup of tea left on top of the machine will hardly move, let alone spill. This characteristic is a measure of the product's:

A conduct

B performance

C consistency

D conformance

E durability

6.25

The salesperson adds that the operating controls are so accurate that water is heated to within one-half degree centigrade of the temperature you set on the selector dial. This characteristic is a measure of the product's:

A conduct

B performance

C consistency

D conformance

E durability

6.26

Service differentiation variables include all of the following except:

A delivery

B reliability

C customer training

D installation

E repair

Case Study 6.2
Tesco's fish counters

In mid-1994, Tesco supermarkets advertised their fish counters in local newspapers in various areas of Britain (see Figure 6.1).

Questions 6.27—6.29 relate to this case study

6.27*

In some areas of Britain, Tesco supermarkets advertised that they carried 68 different types of fish and shellfish, instead of the 42 mentioned in the advertisement. This suggests that:

1 Tesco is positioning itself to compete against other supermarkets selling fish

2 the breadth of Tesco's product mix may vary from place to place

3 some of the stores may be affected by distribution problems

4 the tastes of Tesco customers may vary across the country

5 Tesco is using fish as part of a strategy of enterprise differentiation

A 1 and 2

B 1 and 3

C 2 and 3

D 3 and 4

E 4 and 5

6.28*

In an advertisement in which Tesco advertised 'over 50' different types of fish and shellfish, oysters were pictured instead of swordfish steaks. We may conclude from this that:

1 Tesco's distribution of oysters depends in part on customers' tastes

2 oysters are more expensive per unit weight than swordfish steaks

3 store size in part determines whether oysters are offered

4 the availability of oysters depends in part on the geographic location of the store

5 oysters are not among Tesco's top 42 best-selling seafood items

A 1 and 2

B 1 and 3

C 2 and 3

D 3 and 4

E 4 and 5

6.29

If Tesco wanted to increase its services, it could:

A offer 75 different types of fresh fish and shellfish

B sell pre-packaged fresh seafood products in portions suitable for single servings

C take special orders for fish

D offer samples of cooked or prepared seafood in the store

E offer a double-your-money-back freshness guarantee on its fresh fish

Case Study 6.3
Marketing variables in service advertisements

In 1994, a television advertisement stated that 'you wouldn't perform root canal work after a few lessons from your neighbour,' and, showing a driver and instructor in a British School of Motoring car, suggested that you should take driving lessons from the British School of Motoring, 'the pass masters'. Also in 1994, a television advertisement for United Parcels Service showed the UPS logo circling the globe and stated: 'Our delivery service spans the world. Our promise: predictability. As sure as taking it there yourself.'

Questions 6.30–6.32 relate to this case study

PLAICE

SALMON

SQUID

SWORDFISH STEAKS

Not yet available at Tesco.

HERRINGS

SARDINES

MACKEREL

LARGE PRAWNS

We can however offer you a choice of 42† different types of fish and shellfish.

From the humble Cod to the more exotic Bourgeois from the Seychelles.

Our trained staff will also be happy to prepare it for you, as well as offer recipe and serving suggestions.

And whichever one you choose will be as fresh as the day it was caught.

To see the proof with your own eyes, just visit our new fish counter.

MONKFISH TAIL

Skippingdale Industrial Estate, Scunthorpe.

OPENING HOURS:
Mon-Thur 9am-8pm. Fri 9am-9pm. Sat 8.30am-8pm.
Sunday 10am-4pm.*

TESCO *Every little helps.*

Fig. 6.1 Tesco's fish counters
(reproduced by permission)

6.30*

Comparing the two companies, we observe that:

A both provide a non-goods service

B both provide an owned-goods service

C the British School of Motoring provides a non-goods service, whereas United Parcels Service provides an owned-goods service

D the British School of Motoring provides a rented-goods service, whereas United Parcels Service provides an owned-goods service

E the British School of Motoring provides an owned-goods service, whereas United Parcels Service provides a non-goods service

6.31

The use of which marketing variables is implied in **both** advertisements?

1 product variety

2 warranties

3 product features

4 quality

5 brand name

A 1 and 2

B 1 and 3

C 2 and 3

D 3 and 4

E 4 and 5

6.32

The use of which marketing variables is implied in **only** the United Parcels Service advertisement?

1 product variety

2 warranties

3 product features

4 quality

5 brand name

A 1 and 2

B 1 and 3

C 2 and 3

D 3 and 4

E 4 and 5

6.33

Which of the following statements **incorrectly** distinguishes between the provision of services and the provision of goods?

A services are intangible, whereas goods are tangible

B the quality of many services can be separated from the quality of the service provider, whereas the quality of goods cannot be separated from the quality of the goods provider

C services are usually perishable, whereas goods can be stored

D services are sold first, then produced, whereas goods are usually produced first, then sold

E services may vary in quality over time, whereas goods can be standardized

6.34

Which of the following does **not** explain why the rate of return is higher for high-quality than for low-quality goods firms?

A there are more customers for high-quality goods than for low-quality goods

B high quality tends to generate greater repeat purchasing

C firms offering premium quality can charge premium prices

D high quality usually produces greater consumer loyalty

E word of mouth tends to affect high-quality goods positively and low-quality goods negatively

6.35*

Which is the most appropriate quality strategy to yield the highest return and market share?

A start with superior product quality, and then maintain it

B start with high product quality, and then maintain it

C start with high product quality, and then improve it

D start with average product quality, and then improve it

E start with low product quality, and then improve it

6.36

In the United States, it has been found that many drugs distributed under a trade name have maintained a dominant position in the market even when competitors produce the same item after the 17-year patent protection expires. This suggests that:

A brand positioning largely depends on longevity in the market place

B imitator products usually have lower quality than originals

C the original brand name often acquires important value to the customer

D brands losing their patent protection need not fear competitors

E imitator products usually have fewer features than the originals

6.37*

In assessing a product's quality, which of the following statements are **incorrect**?

1 quality is determined by how well the product meets customer needs and wants

2 high quality results in higher production costs

3 better quality depends on better or higher product specification

4 quality depends on a customer's perception of a product

5 higher pricing is proof of quality

A 1 and 2

B 1 and 3

C 2 and 3

D 3 and 4

E 4 and 5

Case Study 6.4
Marketing small fruit

In autumn 1993, an advertisement for New Zealand apples claimed that the small ones are 'good for kids, good for snacks'. At around the same time, an advertisement for South African Outspan oranges claimed that 'smaller ones are juicier'.

Questions 6.38–6.40 relate to this case study

6.38

The advertisement for New Zealand apples is an example of:

A stimulational marketing

B demarketing

C conversional marketing

D countermarketing

E developmental marketing

6.39*

The marketing tasks in the Outspan oranges advertisement are to:

1 change attitudes towards Outspan

2 add beliefs about small oranges

3 change attitudes towards small oranges

4 change beliefs about small oranges

5 add beliefs about Outspan

A 1 and 2

B 1 and 3

C 2 and 3

D 3 and 4

E 4 and 5

6.40

The common underlying theme in the New Zealand apples and Outspan oranges advertisements is that:

A size does not matter in fruit

B unpopular sizes may have unexpected benefits

C good advertising cannot sell bad products

D there is a trade-off between size and other product characteristics

E a certain amount of exaggeration is permissible to sell unsought goods

6.41

If a manufacturer of a spray deodorant decides to offer a musk fragrance in addition to the original scent, this is a change in product:

A quality

B style

C variety

D branding

E features

6.42

If a manufacturer of spray deodorants decides to produce a roll-on deodorant, this is a change in product:

A quality

B style

C variety

D branding

E features

6.43

In autumn 1993, Dunhill Lights cigarettes changed to a distinctive bevelled-edge pack, suggesting that the package was designed to meet which function?

A ecological

B containment/protection

C usage

D   segmentation

E   communication/promotion

6.44

A manufacturer of motor oil introduces a container with a twist-off top and a pouring spout, suggesting that the package was designed to meet which function?

A   ecological

B   containment/protection

C   usage

D   segmentation

E   communication/promotion

6.45

Many motor oil manufacturers sell their products to European retailers in one-litre and five-litre containers. The most probable reason for this is that:

A   it is difficult for retailers to store more sizes

B   the sizes suit different usage situations

C   it is difficult for retailers to display more sizes

D   the sizes suit different market segments

E   none of these

6.46

A brand of toilet paper is sold in packs of two, four, and nine rolls. The most probable reason for this is that:

A   it is difficult for retailers to store more sizes

B   the sizes suit different usage situations

C   it is difficult for retailers to display more sizes

D   the sizes suit different socio-economic segments

E   none of these

6.47*

From time to time, Kellogg advertises that it does not manufacture breakfast cereals for anyone else. This suggests that Kellogg wants to:

1   protect the Kellogg quality image

2   protect Kellogg's price positioning

3   attack market challengers

4   protect the Kellogg brand name

5   counteract similar package design by competitors

A   1 and 2

B   1 and 3

C   2 and 3

D   3 and 4

E   4 and 5

Case Study 6.5
Micro/ultra washing powders

In spring 1994, a chain of British supermarkets carried ten branded and three own brand micro/ultra washing powders in 2 kg size, as set out in Table 6.2. The powders were of three types: biological, biological for colours, and non-biological. All of these micro/ultra powders promised twice the cleaning power of the same brand's ordinary powder.

Ariel Ultra was offered as a refill pack, inside a special promotional re-usable metal box container that also held a scoop for the powder and a special powder dispenser to put inside the washing machine. The other brands were offered in sturdy cardboard boxes, and it was unclear whether they contained a scoop or dispenser. Fluorescent-coloured boxes were used for Radion (the innovator here) and Daz, while the other brands used more conventional colours. Ariel and Radion biological powders were both discounted from their usual price of £4.79. All brands were also available as soft-package refill packs at about a 45p discount on the hard-package price. Moreover, Daz refill packs came with free Lenor fabric softener refills worth £1.15.

Questions 6.48–6.50 relate to this case study

6.48

Ariel's package may accomplish all of the following **except**:

A   become an integral part of the product itself

B   simplify comparisons between brands

C   establish brand identity

D   reduce production costs

E   act as a surrogate for other product information

6.49*

Daz has a 'look' similar to Radion, but Radion's main rival has been Ariel, the market leader. Meanwhile, an advertising campaign had begun for Daz, telling consumers to 'check it out against own brands: Daz whites cost less than you think'. Looking at all the products on offer, we can infer that Procter & Gamble's strategy is to:

1   make Daz into Radion's main rival

2   protect Ariel with a flanking defence

3   develop a product for each market segment

4   attack Radion in a pincer movement

5   replace product competition with package competition

Table 6.2 Micro/ultra washing powders

Type/name	Manufacturer	Special features/claims	Price for 2 kg container
Biological powders			
Ariel Ultra	Procter & Gamble	metal box container, scoop and dispenser; removes tough oily stains at low temperatures	£3.99
Bold Ultra	Procter & Gamble	two fresh fragrances	£4.79
Daz Ultra	Procter & Gamble	fluorescent red box; removes oily stains at low temperatures	£4.15
Persil Micro System	Lever	promises better cleaning	£4.79
Radion Micro Plus	Lever	fluorescent orange and yellow box; removes stale odours and greasy dirt at low temperatures	£3.99
Supermarket own brand			£3.99
Biological powders for colours			
Ariel Colour	Procter & Gamble	removes tough oily stains at low temperatures	£4.79
Daz Colour	Procter & Gamble	brightest colours at a price that's right	£4.15
Persil Colour	Lever	advanced colour cleaning	£4.79
Supermarket own brand			£3.89
Non-biological powders			
Fairy Ultra	Procter & Gamble	Royal Warrant on box; promises a clean fresh wash, soft next to your family's skin	£4.79
Persil Micro System	Lever	promises better cleaning without damaging colours	£4.79
Supermarket own brand			£3.69 for refill pack

A 1 and 2

B 1 and 3

C 2 and 3

D 3 and 4

E 4 and 5

6.50*

The box of Fairy Ultra discretely bears the Royal Warrant, consisting of the Queen's coat of arms and the statement, 'By appointment to Her Majesty the Queen, manufacturers of soap and detergents, Procter & Gamble Ltd.' Although they could, none of the other Procter & Gamble washing powders carry the Royal Warrant. Lever does not hold a Royal Warrant. Which of the following statements are correct?

1 the use of the warrant may encourage symbolic purchasing behaviour

2 linking the warrant to the brand is a form of instrumental conditioning

3 the warrant is part of the augmented product but not the tangible product

4 the warrant indicates that Fairy is better than Persil

5 use of the warrant is probably more in keeping with Fairy's product positioning than with that of Daz, Bold, or Ariel

A 1 and 2

B 1 and 3

C 2 and 3

D 3 and 4

E 4 and 5

7

NEW PRODUCT DEVELOPMENT

7.1
Which of the following is the **least** justifiable reason for a manufacturer to develop a new product?

A   to utilize excess production capacity

B   to overcome obsolescence of existing products resulting from changes in technology

C   to diversify into new markets

D   to cope with changes in consumer tastes

E   to take advantage of an increase in the size of a target market

7.2*
Which of these types of new products is the odd one out?

A   product-class extensions

B   product-line extensions

C   revised/improved products

D   repositioned products

E   cost-reduced products

7.3*
In the development of new products, a manufacturer's investment risk tends to increase:

1   as the buyer's perception of product newness increases

2   the more dissimilar the new product's technology is from that of existing products

3   the more mature the product market being targeted

4   the greater the cost reductions achieved in manufacturing

5   the more dissimilar the new product's market is from that of the manufacturer's existing products

A   1 and 2

B   1 and 3

C   2 and 3

D   3 and 4

E   4 and 5

7.4*
Which pair of new-product types represents the **greatest** investment risk to a manufacturer?

A   revised/improved products and product-class extensions

B   completely innovative products and repositioned products

C   product-line extensions and revised/improved products

D   product-class extensions and completely innovative products

E   repositioned products and reduced-cost products

7.5
If your company has decided on a new-product strategy to counter-attack a competitor whose newly launched product, incorporating a new feature, has eroded your market share, the most appropriate medium-term policy would be to:

A   develop an entirely new product

B   revise/improve your existing product

C   develop a product-class extension

D   reposition your existing product

E   develop a product-line extension

7.6
Which product-development strategy would be **least** appropriate for a manufacturer of men's spray-on deodorant who wishes to challenge the market leader?

A   add a new range of sizes for existing products

B   add new fragrances to the product line

C   change the packaging of existing products

D   change the brand name

E   add a roll-on range

7.7
Which of the following correctly identify advantages of developing an entirely new product compared with repositioning an existing product in the same product class?

1 it is usually easier to position an entirely new product than to reposition an existing product

2 the success rate of entirely new products is higher than that of repositioned products

3 entirely new products usually provide a longer-term growth and profit potential than repositioned products

4 it is usually cheaper to develop an entirely new product than to reposition an existing product

5 entirely new products can offer new benefits, whereas repositioned products cannot

A 1 and 2

B 1 and 3

C 2 and 3

D 3 and 4

E 4 and 5

7.8
Which of the following correctly identify advantages of revising/improving a product compared with developing an entirely new product in the same product class?

1 revised/improved products generally have a lower likelihood of being pre-empted by new or improved products than have entirely new products

2 revising/improving a product is often more cost-effective than developing an entirely new product

3 the launch costs of revised/improved products tend to be lower than for entirely new products

4 revised/improved products are less subject to price competition than are entirely new products

5 revised/improved products benefit by being more familiar to consumers than entirely new products

A 1 and 2

B 1 and 3

C 2 and 3

D 3 and 4

E 4 and 5

7.9*
If an industry sells low involvement frequently purchased products across a wide range of product categories, we would expect to find:

A moderate product modification and limited new product development

B extensive product modification and limited new product development

C limited product modification and limited new product development

D extensive product modification and extensive new product development

E limited product modification and moderate new product development

7.10*
A study found that for health and beauty aids sold in American grocery shops in 1981, 38 per cent of brands with sales exceeding $1 million, and 50 per cent of brands with sales of $2.5 million to $5 million, were new since 1970. These figures suggest that:

A the creation of entirely new products is more profitable than product modification where opportunities for technological innovation are limited

B the product life cycle of health and beauty aids is relatively short

C the success rate for new health and beauty products is higher than for other new products sold in American grocery shops

D health and beauty brands launched since 1970 have tended to be more closely targeted to markets than older brands have been

E none of these

7.11*
A recent study found that more than 50 per cent of new-product introductions in the United States were either product-line extensions or revisions/improvements of existing products. It is reasonable to infer from this that the majority of new-product introductions:

A follow a low investment risk strategy

B are designed without research and development

C rely to some extent on consumer familiarity with the product

D seek to improve product quality

E follow a pronounced market development strategy

7.12
In the new-product planning process, the first business analysis of the proposal's attractiveness should come immediately before:

A product development

B concept testing

C idea generation

D test marketing

E marketing strategy development

7.13

Which of the following comparisons is **not** part of the business analysis process?

A determination of whether the product's proposed image satisfies the company's objectives

B determination of whether the product's sales projections satisfy the company's objectives

C determination of whether the product's cost projections satisfy the company's objectives

D determination of whether the product's profit projections satisfy the company's objectives

E determination of whether the product's margin projections satisfy the company's objectives

7.14

Which factor would **not** be considered as part of a review and projection of a new product's demand?

A price/sales relationship

B short- and long-run sales potential

C distribution intensity

D likely competitive strategies in response to the new product

E seasonality

7.15*

Which factor would **not** be considered as part of a review and projection of a new product's profitability?

A short- and long-term total and per-unit profits

B time to recoup initial costs

C risk

D return on investment

E break-even point

7.16

The great reduction in recent years in the number of product ideas required to market one successful product (a fall from an average of 58 in 1968 to 7 in 1981) can be attributed to which factors?

1 a decline in the organizational role of the product champion

2 idea-screening procedures have become more effective

3 product-planning methods have improved

4 consumer markets in particular have become less discriminating in relation to new products

5 there has been a shortage of good new-product ideas

A 1 and 2

B 1 and 3

C 2 and 3

D 3 and 4

E 4 and 5

7.17

New-product ideas are **not** usually associated with which of the following sources?

A competitors' products

B company sales representatives

C advertising agencies

D customer complaint letters

E all of these are sources of new-product ideas

7.18*

Which of the following are **inappropriate** as screening questions for a product idea?

1 how large should the product be?

2 how would the product be used?

3 where is the market located?

4 how well-capitalized are potential competitors?

5 do we have the technical capability to design the product?

A 1 and 2

B 1 and 3

C 2 and 3

D 3 and 4

E 4 and 5

7.19

The difference between a product idea and a product concept is that:

A a product idea relates to the characteristics of a product the company might produce, whereas the product concept relates to a product's market-oriented benefits

B a product idea defines the product class of a product, whereas a product concept defines the physical characteristics of a product

C a product idea relates to a product that is entirely new, whereas a product concept relates to a product that has already appeared in one form or another

D a product idea defines the production requirements of a product, whereas a product concept defines the product's market focus

E a product idea is a speculative suggestion to produce a product, whereas a product concept is a properly costed concrete proposal to produce a product

7.20*

Which of the following questions is **inappropriate** for product-concept testing?

A how much do you think the product should sell for?

B how would you expect to learn about the product's availability?

C what colour should the product be?

D when do you think the product should be launched?

E none of the questions is inappropriate for product-concept testing

7.21

Which of the following does **not** represent a benefit of product-concept testing?

A it indicates at an early stage those products likely to be unprofitable if commercialized

B it can help identify desirable modifications to the concept prior to product development

C it saves money by reducing the number of products that would otherwise go to the research and development stage

D it eliminates the need for market testing

E it indicates at an early stage those products likely to be unpopular if commercialized

7.22

The greater the gap between consumer satisfaction with a product concept on one hand and dissatisfaction with existing products on the other:

A the greater the expected purchase frequency of the developed new product

B the greater the risk in developing the new product

C the more we would expect to have to spend on new-product development

D the greater the expected consumer interest in the developed new product

E the greater the perceived value of the new product

7.23

Which of the following is **unnecessary** in establishing a unique selling proposition (USP) for a new product?

A the USP must be presented in a way that establishes brand identity

B the difference must be recognizable by consumers

C the difference must be relevant to consumer needs or wants

D consumers must believe that the new product will deliver the USP it promises

E the difference must convey a cost advantage to the manufacturer

7.24

Which of the following comparisons between consumer testing and market testing of a new product is **inaccurate**?

A consumer testing is done while the product is still being developed, whereas market testing is done once the product has been developed

B consumer testing investigates the degree to which benefits described in the product concept are delivered, whereas market testing investigates how the product performs under realistic market conditions

C consumer testing spreads investigations over a relatively wide geographical area, whereas market testing confines investigations to a relatively smaller area

D the product is not for sale in consumer testing, whereas the product is for sale in market testing

E none of these

7.25*

Which of the following is **not** an objective of test marketing?

A to see how well the product performs in the marketplace against competing brands

B to evaluate marketing strategy before national introduction

C to project sales and revenues to the national market from the test market

D to identify the target market

E to find and correct any weaknesses in the product

7.26*

Which of the following would **not** be a disadvantage of full-scale testing of a product in a large metropolitan area such as London?

A the demographic characteristics of the population may not reflect those of the national market

B advertising for the product may spill out into markets where the product is not being tested

C market share for competitive brands may not be close to the national average

D availability and choice of media may not be representative of the rest of the country

E the size of the area may make the test costs prohibitive

7.27*

The main differences between controlled market tests and full-scale market tests are that:

1 in controlled tests, distribution of the product is limited to specific stores within identified geographical areas, whereas in full-scale tests, distribution of the product is on a widespread basis within identified geographical areas

2 in controlled tests, customers who initially try the product at no cost are re-offered the product at slightly reduced prices, whereas with full-scale tests, no price inducements are given

3 in controlled tests, the research team controls such in-store handling matters as shelf location, number of facings, displays, and in-store promotions, whereas in full-scale tests, these matters are largely left to the retailers

4 in controlled tests, what advertising there is in the test area tends to be limited, whereas in full-scale tests, a full advertising campaign is mounted in the test area

5 in controlled tests, selected panels of shoppers are used to test advertising effectiveness, brand preferences, and re-purchase intentions, whereas in full-scale tests, shoppers are not pre-selected and research focuses on the purchase and re-purchase rate of the product

A 1 and 2

B 1 and 3

C 2 and 3

D 3 and 4

E 4 and 5

7.28

A manufacturer could be justified **not** to market test a new product if the product is:

1 successful in another country

2 intended for frequent purchase

3 easily copied

4 backed by an intensive personal-selling campaign

5 geared to mass distribution

A 1 and 2

B 1 and 3

C 2 and 3

D 3 and 4

E 4 and 5

7.29

When it is used, test marketing of industrial products usually takes the form of:

1 product-use tests

2 sales-wave research

3 trade-show exhibitions

4 simulated test research

5 distributor and dealer display-room exhibitions

A 1 and 2

B 1 and 3

C 2 and 3

D 3 and 4

E 4 and 5

7.30

Which of the following is **not** a drawback associated with market testing?

A market testing cannot pre-test alternative marketing plans

B market testing can cause delays in getting the product fully established in the market

C market testing may reveal actions to the competition prematurely

D market testing cannot take account of such external factors as changes in the economy

E all of these are drawbacks

7.31

Which of the following is an **inappropriate** criterion for rating the attractiveness of alternative markets for a new-product introduction?

A market potential

B company's local reputation

C competitive penetration

D cost of filling the pipeline

E none of these is inappropriate

7.32

The new-product rollout strategy for a leading manufacturer of instant coffee usually differs from that of a leading manufacturer of cars in that:

A the coffee manufacturer will enter only a few cities at a time, whereas the car manufacturer will introduce its products into a whole region and then move to the next region

B the coffee manufacturer will choose step-wise regional introduction, whereas the car manufacturer will launch nationally

C the coffee manufacturer will introduce the product nationally, whereas the car manufacturer will launch internationally

D the coffee manufacturer will enter several regions at first, moving quickly to complete national introduction, whereas the car manufacturer will enter one region at a time, and move less quickly to national introduction

E there is no difference, since both will launch nationally

7.33

In a given market, if a firm intends to achieve parallel entry with a competitor with a similar new product, we would expect to find that:

A the competitor will dictate the firm's launch schedule

B the competitor will bear most of the cost of educating the market

C the firm will save on research and development

D the firm is the market leader

E none of these

7.34*

A product is being introduced under the following conditions: a large part of the potential market is unaware of the product; those who are aware are eager for the product and are willing to pay the asking price; the company faces potential competition and wants to establish brand preference. The best introductory marketing strategy would be:

A slow skimming

B rapid skimming

C slow penetration

D rapid penetration

E cannot be determined from the information provided

7.35*

A product is being introduced under the following conditions: the market is large, highly unaware of the product, and is price-sensitive; there is some potential competition. The best introductory marketing strategy would be:

A slow skimming

B rapid skimming

C slow penetration

D rapid penetration

E cannot be determined from the information provided

7.36*

A product is being introduced under the following conditions: the market is large, highly unaware of the product, and is largely price-sensitive; there is strong potential competition; and the company's unit manufacturing costs fall with the scale of production and accumulated manufacturing experience. The best introductory marketing strategy would be:

A slow skimming

B rapid skimming

C slow penetration

D rapid penetration

E cannot be determined from the information provided

7.37

The chances of a new product's success are enhanced:

1 the greater the product's complexity

2 the more observable the product's attributes or characteristics

3 the easier it is to sample the product before purchase

4 the more completely innovative the product

5 the greater the product's relative advantage over existing competing offerings

A 1 and 2

B 1 and 3

C 2 and 3

D 3 and 4

E 4 and 5

7.38*

If a model of consumer new-product adoption starts with stages of product awareness, information gathering, and product evaluation, we can infer that:

1 complex decision-making is anticipated

2 a low-involvement product is involved

3 adoption will reflect communication within rather than across groups

4 the rate of diffusion will be the same for most consumer products

5 risk reduction is important in the decision-making process

A 1 and 2
B 1 and 3
C 2 and 3
D 3 and 4
E 4 and 5

7.39
In the consumer-adoption process, heavy-user target marketing is appropriate only when:

1 most people are potential buyers
2 the heavy users are identifiable
3 most of the heavy users are early adopters
4 most of the heavy users are not brand loyal
5 the mass market approach has been tried and has failed

A 1 and 2
B 1 and 3
C 2 and 3
D 3 and 4
E 4 and 5

7.40
Which of the following statements about product innovators is **untrue**?

A innovators in a given product class tend to be heavy users

B innovators are relatively easily reached by various forms of promotion and non-commercial communication

C innovators in one product class are most likely to be innovators in many broadly different product classes

D innovators tend to be opinion leaders

E innovators are the people who must be reached first by company promotional efforts

7.41
Which of the following **inaccurately** portrays a difference between innovators on one hand, and late adopters on the other?

A innovators tend to have higher incomes than late adopters

B innovators tend to be more reliant on group norms than late adopters

C innovators tend to be better educated than late adopters

D innovators tend to be more active outside their community than late adopters

E none of these

7.42
Which of the following correctly portrays early adopters?

A early adopters almost invariably come from the higher social classes

B early adopters almost invariably come from the middle social classes

C early adopters almost invariably come from the lower social classes

D early adopters almost invariably come from a mixture of social classes

E early adopters can come from any given segment of society, depending on the innovation

7.43*
Which of the following is **not** a shortcoming of the Rogers product adoption curve?

A it cannot predict how long the adoption period will be

B it is impossible in practice to design marketing mixes to reach each of the identified adoption groups

C it does not account for non-adopters

D the predicted shape of the adoption curve often does not match the shape of the adoption curve in reality

E it is arbitrary in determining the characteristics of each adoption group

7.44*
Since the 1970s, which of the following has **not** been a contributing factor to the increasing importance of the trickle across effect in new-product introduction in North America and Western Europe?

A the quick dissemination of information through the mass media

B the persistence of relatively sharp class distinctions

C increased consumer purchasing power

D the social multiplier effect

E none of these

7.45
A manufacturer in the mid-1990s wishing to encourage the trickle down effect for a new perfume might adopt a marketing strategy that included:

1 regular full-page advertisements in leading high-fashion magazines

2 television advertisements featuring a model in her mid-twenties, surrounded by several male admirers attracted by her perfume

3 a brand name suggesting royal or aristocratic connections (e.g. Contessa)

4 endorsement by a well-known female pop star

5 a national poster campaign depicting a dressing table on which is the perfume bottle, a diamond tiara, and, in the background, the suggestion of a framed photograph of HRH The Duke of Edinburgh

A 1 and 2

B 1 and 3

C 2 and 3

D 3 and 4

E 4 and 5

7.46*

Once a new product has been launched and adoption begins to increase, it is typical to find that:

A the innovators stop using the product

B the marketing mix changes to broaden the originally defined target market

C the product requires repositioning

D the laggards start to enter the market

E none of these

7.47

It has been found that in the majority of cases, a company will develop an idea or technology and will then determine if there is a need. This situation need not conflict with the marketing concept so long as:

1 the cost of introduction is less than the cost of consumer testing

2 the development team has successfully followed this procedure before

3 the product has quality superiority over the competition

4 the company tests whether the product meets consumer needs

5 the product is positioned to a defined market segment

A 1 and 2

B 1 and 3

C 2 and 3

D 3 and 4

E 4 and 5

7.48

The owner of a classic car has to replace a brake light cover and finds that the particular part is no longer manufactured. This is an example of:

A planned obsolescence

B physical obsolescence

C technological obsolescence

D fashion obsolescence

E product obsolescence

7.49

An electric razor bought six years ago has broken down and cannot be repaired, necessitating the purchase of a new model. This is an example of:

A planned obsolescence

B physical obsolescence

C technological obsolescence

D fashion obsolescence

E product obsolescence

7.50

A company manufacturing domestic crockery adopts a policy of introducing new patterns every two years and deleting most existing patterns. This is an example of:

A planned obsolescence

B physical obsolescence

C technological obsolescence

D fashion obsolescence

E product obsolescence

8

BRANDS AND BRANDING

8.1

Which of the following conditions are necessary for the successful branding of a product?

1   the product is easy to identify by brand or trademark
2   demand for the general product class is small
3   dependable and widespread distribution is possible
4   product quality is difficult to maintain
5   there are economies of scale

A   1 and 2
B   1 and 3
C   2 and 3
D   3 and 4
E   4 and 5

8.2*

Which of the following statements **incorrectly** portrays an advantage of brand competition over price competition?

A   price cuts can be easily matched by rivals quickly, whereas brand and advertising changes take time to match
B   branding allows the changing of customary price levels without affecting demand
C   price changes are more obvious than brand changes to customers
D   price rises can be disguised by brand improvements or other promotions
E   price reductions may be associated with real or perceived quality reductions

8.3

The difference between a brand mark and a trademark is that:

A   a brand mark is a symbol or design associated with a brand, whereas the trademark is the brand's name
B   a brand mark is a symbol or design associated with a brand, whereas a trademark is the legal protection given to the exclusive use of a brand mark

C   a brand mark is the brand name written in a distinctive way, whereas a trademark is a symbol or sign associated with the brand
D   a brand mark is the legal protection given to the exclusive use of a brand name, whereas a trademark is the brand name written in a distinctive way
E   a brand mark is the brand name of the company, whereas a trademark is the legal protection given to the exclusive use of the brand name

8.4

Which of the following is **not** a function of a brand name?

A   simplification of the selection process
B   a tendency to promote brand loyalty
C   maximization of the amount of information available to the customer
D   differentiation of one product from a similar one
E   all of these are functions of a brand name

8.5*

An important difference between a private brand, a distributor brand, and an own brand is that:

A   private and distributor brands are designed entirely by the manufacturer, whereas the seller determines the design of own brands
B   there is essentially no difference, in that all three terms relate to a manufacturer placing the brand name of a retailer or non-retailer intermediary on a product
C   private brands are sold only by retailers; distributor brands are sold only by non-retailer intermediaries; and own brands are sold by either retailers or non-retailer intermediaries
D   private brands tend to have more elaborate and distinctive packaging than own brands, and both have more elaborate and distinctive packaging than distributor brands
E   generally, the quality of private brands is higher than that of own brands, and both have higher quality than distributor brands

8.6*

Which of the following is **not** an advantage to a manufacturer who supplies both manufacturer and distributor brands?

A there are economies of scale through raw material purchasing, distribution, and production

B substantial sales may result with minimal promotional or selling costs

C it can provide a base for expansion

D if a manufacturer does not supply distributor brands, the competitors will, possibly strengthening the competitors' cost structure

E the market is increased without endangering sales of the manufacturer brand

8.7*

In relation to customer typologies associated with different types of brands, which of the following comparisons are accurate?

1 customers preferring manufacturer brands tend to spend less time on comparison shopping than those who prefer generic brands

2 customers preferring manufacturer brands usually seek the same quality as those who prefer generic brands

3 customers preferring own brands are usually more price conscious than those who prefer generic brands

4 customers preferring manufacturer brands tend to be brand loyal, whereas those preferring own brands tend to be store loyal

5 customers preferring manufacturer brands tend to be risk avoiders, whereas those preferring own brands tend to be moderate risk takers

A 1 and 2

B 1 and 3

C 2 and 3

D 3 and 4

E 4 and 5

8.8*

Which of the following comparisons between types of brands are accurate?

1 manufacturer brands tend to have deeper product lines than own brands

2 neither own brands nor generic brands are usually advertised

3 manufacturer brands are usually sold by many competing dealers, whereas own brands are usually available only in outlets of a single firm

4 the brand image of own brands and generic brands is usually the same

5 own brands usually have more emphasis on packaging than generic brands

A 1 and 2

B 1 and 3

C 2 and 3

D 3 and 4

E 4 and 5

8.9

Which of the following statements **incorrectly** compare own brands with manufacturer/national brands?

1 own brands are usually cheaper than manufacturer brands

2 product quality of own brands is usually as good or better than that of manufacturer brands

3 own brands can contribute to a store's enterprise differentiation, whereas manufacturer brands cannot

4 margins on own brands tend to be higher than those on manufacturer brands

5 own brands are more closely targeted to market segments than are manufacturer brands

A 1 and 2

B 1 and 3

C 2 and 3

D 3 and 4

E 4 and 5

8.10

When Kellogg cereals advertises that it does not make cereals for any other company, it is trying to protect its:

A product differentiation

B brand name

C brand image

D trademark

E product patents

8.11

Xerox has advertised that 'there is no such thing as a xerox, you can't make a xerox, you can't go to the xerox,' but adds that 'on the other hand, you can make copies on the Xerox copier, you can go to the Xerox copier, and you can read a Xerox textbook'. Such a statement indicates that:

A Xerox is trying to reposition its brand name

B Xerox wants to prevent its brand name from becoming generic

C Xerox is trying to broaden the product classes associated with its brand name

D Xerox wants to target new market segments

E none of these

8.12

Some large retailers have created several brand names to identify related products (e.g., DieHard batteries, Craftsman tools, and Kenmore appliances, which are brand names created by Sears). This is an example of which branding strategy?

A generic branding

B combined branding

C specific product branding

D product line branding

E manufacturer branding

8.13

If a firm decides not to designate a brand name on a product in order to offer a lower-price option to buyers, which branding strategy is being used?

A generic branding

B combined branding

C specific product branding

D product line branding

E manufacturer branding

8.14

When a manufacturer assigns different brand names to its different products, which branding strategy is being used?

A generic branding

B combined branding

C specific product branding

D product line branding

E manufacturer branding

8.15

The practice of a large retailer creating several brand names to identify different quality products within the same product class (e.g. A & P food stores' Ann Page,

Sultana, and Iona set of brands) is an example of which branding strategy?

A generic branding

B combined branding

C specific product branding

D product line branding

E manufacturer branding

8.16*

When a manufacturer has a strong corporate identity and views its products within the context of a total product mix rather than as independent profit centres, which branding strategy is most advisable?

A generic branding

B combined branding

C specific product branding

D product line branding

E manufacturer branding

8.17*

When a manufacturer has a strong corporate identity and views its products as independent profit centres rather than within the context of a total product mix, which branding strategy is most advisable?

A generic branding

B combined branding

C specific product branding

D product line branding

E manufacturer branding

8.18*

Combined branding is usually **least** effective for which kinds of goods?

1 inexpensive goods

2 high involvement goods

3 frequently purchased goods

4 goods whose purchase requires group consultation/ decision

5 goods from disparate product categories

A 1 and 2

B 1 and 3

C 2 and 3

D 3 and 4

E 4 and 5

Case Study 8.1
Generic supermarket brands

In the late 1970s and early 1980s, some British supermarket chains were encouraged by Carrefour's initial success in introducing generic products in France, and decided to follow in the UK. In the relatively harsh economic climate of the time, there was growing consumer scepticism about the price premium being paid for branding. Indeed, many supermarket own brands were doing well, and their quality was gradually improving. Generics were seen as a popular alternative to manufacturer brands.

The tendency was to give the generic range a name (e.g., BASICS at Argyll, Plain and Simple at International Stores, and Value Lines at Tesco), develop distinctive packs, and heavily promote their introduction. The generic ranges were typically priced 40 per cent lower on average than the equivalent own brand. Profit margins, and also quality, were lower than for equivalent own brands. In the event, consumers began to think of generics as an extension of own labels, and therefore switched from own brands to generics. All the generic ranges were withdrawn in Britain by the end of 1988.

Questions 8.19–8.20 relate to this case study

8.19

In terms of the concept of generics:

A the price difference between the generic and the manufacturer brands should have been larger than it was in practice

B middle-class ambivalence towards consumption, upon which the attraction of generics rests, is strongest during periods of prosperity, suggesting that the timing of the launches was wrong

C the ranges, as they were introduced in practice, were not true generics

D since the appeal of generics depends on brand perception, which differs internationally, their introduction in the UK was unwise

E none of these

8.20

The history of generic branding in British supermarkets illustrates that:

1 brands that do not generate sufficient profits become liabilities

2 insufficient resources were invested in the generic branding strategy

3 multibranding can lead to cannibalization

4 inappropriate names can cause the failure of brands

5 a company's corporate image is liable to be affected by the brands it stocks

A 1 and 2

B 1 and 3

C 2 and 3

D 3 and 4

E 4 and 5

8.21

A manufacturer's strategy of brand proliferation provides all of the following advantages **except**:

A acting as a barrier to market entry by competitors

B improving the manufacturer's claim to shelf space

C allowing more precise targeting of markets

D facilitating overall market share maximization

E preventing cannibalization of the manufacturer's leading brand

Case Study 8.2
Branding electrical goods

A manufacturer of electrical goods produces products that tend to fall into three quality categories. For example, its televisions, portable radios, and hair dryers are of superior quality; its electric shavers, washing machines, and toasters are of average quality; and its telephones, vacuum cleaners, and dishwashers are of below average quality.

Questions 8.22 and 8.23 relate to this case study

8.22*

If this manufacturer were to use the same brand name for all of its products, what level of quality would most people be likely to expect on seeing the brand name?

A low level

B medium level

C high level

D they would be unable to form an opinion

E the question cannot be answered with the information provided

8.23*

If this company wanted to maximize brand impact, it would be advised to:

A family brand all of its products

B adopt individual brand names for all of its products

C develop separate family brand names to reflect quality levels

D use a manufacturer's brand for the superior products, and distributors' brands for the others

E use the same manufacturer's brand for the superior and average products, and a distributor's brand for the weaker products

8.24*

A strong emphasis on branding (as in the prominent use of the brand name) is advisable when:

A other manufacturers have smaller advertising budgets

B the manufacturer is not well-known

C the product is not well-known

D there is product proliferation

E sales begin to fall below planned levels

8.25

If a car manufacturer introduces a new sports model under its company brand name, this is an example of:

A a brand extension

B brand development

C brand equity

D brand repositioning

E flanker branding

8.26

If a car manufacturer markets a range of casual clothing under its company brand name, this is an example of:

A a brand extension

B brand development

C brand equity

D brand repositioning

E flanker branding

8.27

If a manufacturer of lawnmowers introduces a hedge trimmer under a new brand name, this is an example of:

A a brand extension

B brand development

C brand equity

D brand repositioning

E flanker branding

8.28

If a manufacturer of toothpastes introduces a dispenser gel toothpaste under a new brand name, this is an example of:

A a brand extension

B brand development

C brand equity

D brand repositioning

E flanker branding

8.29

Which test would be **inappropriate** in determining the brand name to be used for a new product?

A association test

B graphics test

C pronunciation test

D recall test

E preference test

8.30*

Which of the following is **not** considered a benefit of an individual brand strategy?

A the more brands a manufacturer has, the more highly a consumer regards the firm

B offering several brands facilitates capturing 'brand switchers'

C the more successful brands that manufacturers have, the greater the retailer's dependence on their brands

D creating new brands tends to develop excitement and efficiency within the manufacturer's organization

E an individual brand strategy positions each brand to capture a different market segment

8.31

In which situation would a brand-extension strategy be **inadvisable**?

A when the original product is developed in a different form

B when a new product is to express the same expertise as the original brand

C when there is a different customer franchise for a new product

D when a new product is to express the same image/status as the original brand

E when a new optional feature is added to the original product

8.32

Which of the following statements is **untrue** of brand extensions?

A a brand extension gives a new product instant recognition

B a brand extension that disappoints a consumer may hurt the consumer's regard for the company's other products

C all the advertising costs to familiarize consumers with the new name are saved

D frequent use of a brand name may cause the individual products to lack impact or personality compared with individual brands

E brand extensions are best employed when there are sizeable differences between the new and current products in terms of features, benefits, quality, or price

8.33

If a company makes major changes to an existing brand to appeal to a broader market, it is engaging in:

A brand reinforcement

B brand integration

C brand development

D brand repositioning

E brand modification

8.34

If a company seeks to market an existing brand to new segments, it is engaging in:

A brand reinforcement

B brand integration

C brand development

D brand repositioning

E brand modification

8.35*

It is most common to find brand loyalty for a product when:

A consumer involvement with the product is high and complex/extended decision-making is involved

B consumer involvement with the product is low and limited decision-making is involved

C consumer involvement with the product is high and limited decision-making is involved

D consumer involvement with the product is low and habitual decision-making is involved

E consumer involvement with the product is high and habitual decision-making is involved

8.36

All things being equal, the most successful outcome of a new brand introduction for a firm will be that the new brand:

A takes sales from the firm's current brands without expanding the market

B takes sales from the firm's current brands and the competitors' brands and brings new buyers into the market

C takes sales from the competitors' brands and brings new buyers into the market

D takes sales from the firm's current brands and the competitors' brands without expanding the market

E takes sales from the firm's current brands and brings new buyers into the market

8.37*

Which of the following characteristics would **not** usually be associated with a brand loyal customer (i.e. a customer displaying loyalty to brands in a considerable number of product classes):

A relatively little time for shopping

B relatively large amounts of discretionary time available for shopping

C a perception of small interbrand differences in quality

D a reliance on package and advertising information

E a concern with receiving value for money

8.38

Advertising for a company aiming to reinforce brand loyalty ought to:

A compare the brand with other brands

B concentrate on product information

C frequently repeat the message

D associate product benefits with consumer needs

E vary the message frequently

8.39

An American survey in 1989 found that 12 per cent of consumers were not loyal to any brand for the twenty-five product types tested, 47 per cent were brand loyal for one to five product types, and only two per cent were brand loyal for more than sixteen product types. From this it can be concluded that:

A the proportion of brand loyal customers in the population is no longer large enough to justify branding

B brand loyalty is associated with certain psychological characteristics

C those who are brand loyal tend to be the heavy users of the product types

D brand loyalty has declined since the 1970s

E none of these

8.40
In terms of the percentage of users of a given product type who are loyal to one brand, the greatest brand loyalty would be expected for:

A domestic batteries

B gasoline

C soft drinks

D cigarettes

E televisions

8.41*
Which of the following statements accurately compares the behavioural with the cognitive approach to the study of brand loyalty?

A the behavioural approach views brand loyalty as both a function of and consequence of consistently purchasing one brand over time, whereas the cognitive approach views brand loyalty as a function of consumer characteristics, brand attitudes, and consumer needs

B the behavioural approach believes that consumer price sensitivity determines brand loyalty, whereas the cognitive approach believes that a strong stimulus-response link determines it

C the behavioural approach holds that brand loyalty is a function of psychological processes, whereas the cognitive approach holds that it is a function of evaluative processes

D the behavioural approach believes that brand loyalty reflects brand satisfaction and reinforcement, whereas the cognitive approach believes that brand loyalty reflects decision-making processes

E none of these

Case Study 8.3
Brand switching

A consumer who has been brand loyal to Douwe Egbert Dutch filter coffee noticed that Van Nelle Dutch filter coffee, which normally costs as much as Douwe Egbert in the supermarket, offered a 'three for the price of two' deal. She therefore bought three packages of Van Nelle. After they were finished, she bought another three packages of Van Nelle on offer. When this coffee was consumed, she returned to the supermarket to find that Van Nelle's offer had ended, and bought Douwe Egbert coffee once more.

Questions 8.42–8.44 relate to this case study

8.42
This consumer's behaviour reflects which purchasing pattern?

A reinforcement

B vacillation

C reversion

D experimentation

E conversion

8.43
On her next visit to the supermarket, she bought a package of Lyon's Continental blend filter coffee, costing as much as Douwe Egbert and Van Nelle. Her behaviour now reflects which purchasing pattern?

A reinforcement

B vacillation

C reversion

D experimentation

E conversion

8.44*
The marketing strategy **least** likely to induce a brand loyal consumer to switch brands is for the competing brand to:

A try to simplify the choice process

B advertise a new feature in an existing brand

C try to change consumer priorities by stressing an existing feature that consumers had not previously considered

D offer free product samples

E introduce a line extension of an existing brand that offers a new benefit

8.45*
Which of the following objectives are usually associated with a manufacturer's goal to establish a strong brand franchise?

1 to change the occasional purchaser of its brand to a repeat purchaser

2 to control advertising and promotional expenditure so that the brand will be price competitive with rivals

3 where possible to increase the amount consumed by repeat purchasers of its brand

4 to develop new brands to challenge competitors

5 to attract purchasers from competing brands

A 1 and 2

B 1 and 3

C 2 and 3

D 3 and 4

E 4 and 5

8.46

Which of the following is **not** a factor influencing successful brand strategy?

A the level of market maturity

B a sales-based incentive system within the manufacturer's organization

C the identification of retailers' objectives

D understanding consumer motives for buying a brand

E an analysis of potential competition

8.47*

Which of the following statements correctly identify differences between consumer market branding and organizational/industrial market branding?

1 there is usually a greater emphasis on emotional aspects in consumer branding than in organizational branding

2 suppliers give more commitment to consumer brands than to organizational brands

3 the name of the company more commonly appears as part of the brand name in organizational brands than in consumer brands

4 brand names tend to be more functional in organizational branding than in consumer branding

5 there is a greater propensity towards brand loyalty in industrial markets than in consumer markets

A 1 and 2

B 1 and 3

C 2 and 3

D 3 and 4

E 4 and 5

8.48

Which of these brand names has the greatest company association?

A Cadbury's Dairy Milk

B Ariel

C British Telecom

D Sainsbury's Baked Beans

E Kit Kat from Rowntree

8.49

Which of these brand names has the least company association?

A Cadbury's Dairy Milk

B Ariel

C British Telecom

D Sainsbury's Baked Beans

E Kit Kat from Rowntree

8.50*

In the late 1980s, a number of established producers of wood and plywood panels in the United States were faced with increasing competition from new entrants. They decided that the best way to counter this threat was to adopt the branding strategy of developing names for their lines. Several months later, the majority of timber merchants interviewed in a survey claimed that their first consideration in deciding on wood suppliers was price. This suggests that:

A consumers were confused by the brand names

B the producers failed to differentiate their products in terms of their added values

C branding is inappropriate for this class of products

D the timber merchants no longer regarded the competing products as commodities

E none of these

9

PRODUCT LIFE CYCLE (PLC)

9.1*

The concept underlying that of the product life cycle (PLC) is the:

A product-form life cycle

B brand life cycle

C demand life cycle

D demand-technology life cycle

E technology life cycle

9.2

The shortest life cycle history will normally be for:

A product categories

B needs

C technology

D product forms

E brands

9.3

The longest life cycle will normally be for:

A product categories

B needs

C technology

D product forms

E brands

9.4

Which of the following are **not** product forms?

1 cordless telephones

2 16-bit notepad PCs

3 cigarettes

4 open-top 4-wheel drive cars

5 microwave ovens

A 1 and 2

B 1 and 3

C 2 and 3

D 3 and 4

E 4 and 5

9.5*

In the course of the technological change of a product (e.g. the development of biological washing powders and liquids, and then the creation of concentrated versions) it is common to find that:

1 competitive advantage depends more on cash flow than on having the very latest fashion in technology

2 the cycle is under the control of the supplier, not the market

3 the brand name does not change its place in the market, although the product version does

4 sales volumes of low technology products go into irretrievable decline

5 the product life cycle shortens noticeably

A 1 and 2

B 1 and 3

C 2 and 3

D 3 and 4

E 4 and 5

9.6*

Which of the following comparisons between the market life cycle concept and the product life cycle concept is **incorrect**?

A in some, typically new markets, the pattern of growth of the market follows that of the main brands until maturity is reached

B in some well-established markets, the life cycle of new segments associated with the emergence of major new products tends to parallel that of the new products

C the product life cycle is of most direct significance to the supplier, whereas the market life cycle is likely to be of much more importance to the other participants, especially the retailers

D the market life cycle predicts the shakeout of weaker competitors during the market growth phase, whereas the product life cycle predicts this for the product maturity phase

E the market life cycle predicts saturation as more likely to occur during the market growth phase than the market maturity phase, in contrast to the product life cycle, which views saturation as a feature of the market maturity phase

9.7

The greatest insight into a product's competitive dynamics is gained from analysis of the:

A demand life cycle

B product life cycle

C product-form life cycle

D brand life cycle

E demand-technology life cycle

9.8

The life cycle curve depicting the shift in demand from slide-rules to electronic calculators and then to personal computers would represent the:

A demand life cycle

B product life cycle

C product-form life cycle

D brand life cycle

E demand-technology life cycle

9.9

Which of the following assumptions is **invalid** in relation to the concept of the PLC?

A there are common evolutionary processes which influence markets over time

B the same marketing strategy is appropriate for all products at any given stage of the PLC

C the duration of the life cycle phases can be influenced by managerial action

D the stages of a given PLC are defined by the product's pattern of sales growth

E the concept of the PLC is more relevant to successful than unsuccessful products

9.10

Which of the following is an **improper** use of the PLC?

A to develop specific sales forecasts for a given product

B to anticipate competitive activities

C to form a basis for timing the development and launch of new products

D to re-appraise a product periodically

E to anticipate changes in buyer behaviour

9.11*

At which stages of the PLC would a differentiated product strategy be suitable?

1 introduction

2 growth

3 maturity

4 decline

A 1 and 2

B 1 and 3

C 2 and 3

D 2 and 4

E 3 and 4

9.12

The target customers in the decline stage of the PLC are the:

A innovators

B early adopters

C early majority

D late majority

E laggards

9.13

In the growth stage of the PLC, marketing strategy should concentrate on:

1 pre-empting the competition

2 defending market share

3 cutting costs

4 targeting new segments

5 developing brand image

A 1 and 2

B 1 and 3

C 2 and 3

D 3 and 4

E 4 and 5

9.14*

The implication of the PLC is that expenditure on consumer sales and promotion should be:

A heavy in the introduction phase, moderate in the growth phase, heavy in the maturity phase, and minimal in the decline phase

B heavy in the introduction and growth phases, moderate in the maturity phase, and minimal in the decline phase

C moderate in the introduction phase, heavy in the growth phase, and moderate in the maturity and decline phases

D moderate in the introduction phase, heavy in the growth and maturity phases, and minimal in the decline phase

E heavy in the introduction, growth, and maturity phases, and minimal in the decline phase

9.15*

The implication of the PLC is that advertising expenditure should be:

A heavy in the introduction and growth phases, moderate in the maturity phase, and light in the decline phase

B heavy in the introduction phase, moderate in the growth and maturity phases, and light in the decline phase

C heavy in the introduction, growth, and maturity phases, and moderate in the decline phase

D heavy in the introduction phase, moderate in the growth phase, heavy in the maturity phase, and light in the decline phase

E moderate in the introduction phase, heavy in the growth and maturity phases, and moderate in the decline phase

9.16

A product-extension strategy (such as promoting baking soda as a food-odour absorber for refrigerators as well as an ingredient for baking) usually employs all of the following approaches **except**:

A promoting more frequent usage among current users

B attracting new users

C developing new uses for the basic material

D concentrating on efficiency and cost control

E promoting more varied usage among current users

9.17

The most appropriate time to use a product extension strategy is:

A during the introduction phase

B during the growth phase

C during the growth and maturity phases

D during the maturity phase

E during the decline phase

9.18*

According to PLC theory, the level of profits at the middle of the maturity phase will usually be:

A maintained until the start of the decline stage

B at its highest point

C comparable to the level at the middle of the growth phase

D comparable to the level at the end of the growth phase

E none of these

9.19

According to PLC theory, the fastest rate of growth of profits for a product should occur:

A near the end of the introduction phase

B soon after the start of the growth phase

C near the end of the growth phase

D soon after the start of the maturity phase

E near the end of the maturity phase

9.20

Most products are in what stage of the life cycle?

A introduction

B growth

C maturity

D decline

E cannot be determined

9.21

The growth phase of the PLC is analogous to which concept in the Boston Consulting Group analysis?

A question mark

B star

C cash cow

D dog

E there is no analogous concept

9.22*

The differences between PLC curves of product A and product B in Figure 9.1 suggest that:

A product B will be more profitable than product A over its lifetime

B more money has been spent on promotion for product B than for product A

C product A should be deleted before product B

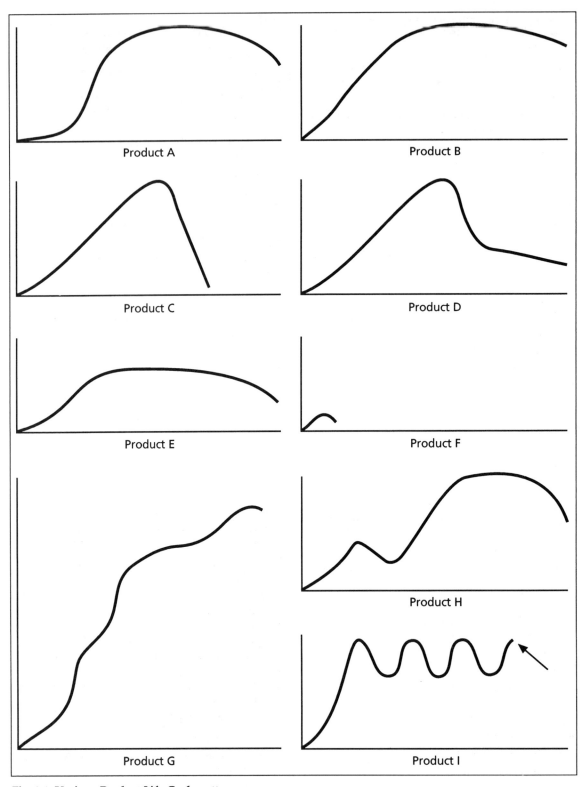

Fig. 9.1 Various Product Life Cycle patterns

D competition was more severe for product A than for product B

E product B is a low-learning product compared with product A

9.23

PLC pattern of product C in Figure 9.1 would be typical for a product such as a:

A skateboard

B Hula-Hoop

C raw material

D Scotch whisky

E Barbie doll

9.24

PLC pattern of product D in Figure 9.1 would be typical for a product such as a:

A skateboard

B Hula-Hoop

C raw material

D Scotch whisky

E Barbie doll

9.25

PLC pattern of product E in Figure 9.1 would be typical for a product such as a:

A skateboard

B Hula-Hoop

C raw material

D Scotch whisky

E Barbie doll

9.26

Product F in Figure 9.1 is at what phase of the PLC?

A introduction

B growth

C maturity

D decline

E cannot be determined

9.27

PLC pattern of product G in Figure 9.1 would be typical for a product such as a:

A skateboard

B Hula-Hoop

C raw material

D Scotch whisky

E Barbie doll

9.28

PLC pattern of product H in Figure 9.1 would be typical for a:

A style

B fad

C fashion

D seasonal product

E none of these

9.29

PLC pattern of product I in Figure 9.1 would be typical for a:

A style

B fad

C fashion

D seasonal product

E none of these

9.30*

If an advertising campaign were to be initiated for product I at the arrowed point, we would expect sales to:

A increase substantially above their present level during the campaign, and return to their present level for an extended period at the conclusion of the campaign

B maintain their present level during the campaign and for an extended period at the conclusion of the campaign

C be relatively unaffected by the campaign, generally following the previous pattern

D maintain their present level for the duration of the campaign, then following a pattern that cannot yet be predicted

E increase above their present level for the duration of the campaign, then following a pattern that cannot yet be predicted

9.31*

Which PLC pattern in Figure 9.1 suggests that a product relaunch or repositioning has occurred?

A product D

B product G

C product H

D product I

E none of these

9.32*

Which PLC pattern in Figure 9.1 suggests that a product-extension strategy has been followed?

A product D

B product G

C product H

D product I

E none of these

9.33

The use of below-the-line promotions such as money-off offers, free gifts, and competitions are most often employed at what stage of a brand's life cycle?

A introduction

B growth

C maturity

D decline

E at all stages

9.34*

The brand strategy most appropriate for the growth phase of the PLC is:

A brand reinforcement

B brand repositioning

C brand development

D brand modification

E brand rejuvenation

9.35*

Brands that last for generations can attribute their longevity to retaining their:

A price positioning

B technological content

C brand values

D design content

E service content

9.36

In launching a new product, the preferred marketing strategy is:

A slow skimming

B rapid skimming

C slow penetration

D rapid penetration

E cannot be determined from the information provided

9.37*

The greatest strategic dangers at the introduction phase of the PLC for the company introducing the product are that:

1 the company will not be able to establish a commanding position before imitators go into the market

2 demand will outstrip supply

3 slow adoption of the product may cause considerable financial problems to the company

4 the early adopters may not like the product

5 the product may not be perceived as new enough to merit a switch in purchasing behaviour

A 1 and 2

B 1 and 3

C 2 and 3

D 3 and 4

E 4 and 5

9.38*

Which of the following marketing strategies would be **inappropriate** in the PLC growth phase?

1 reduce the price

2 concentrate advertising on building product awareness

3 reduce the number of distribution channels

4 add new models

5 improve product quality

A 1 and 2

B 1 and 3

C 2 and 3

D 3 and 4

E 4 and 5

9.39*

Which sales promotion strategy is most appropriate for the growth phase?

A heavy use of promotion to entice trial

B reduce promotion to the level needed to retain hard-core loyals

C increase promotion considerably to encourage brand switching

D maintain or increase promotion slightly over previous levels to meet competition

E discontinue promotion, but keep the situation under review

9.40*

Which of the following tactics are appropriate for a company deciding to harvest a brand?

1 find a buyer for the brand

2 reduce the sales force

3 reposition the product

4 reduce product quality

5 cut research and development

A 1 and 2

B 1 and 3

C 2 and 3

D 3 and 4

E 4 and 5

9.41*

Which marketing strategy would be **inappropriate** in the maturity stage?

A to add new features

B to try to enter new market segments

C to simplify the product

D to reduce the price

E none of these

Case Study 9.1
Servicing older BMW cars

Research in the United Kingdom indicated that as BMW cars became older and passed through successive owners, the likelihood increased that the cars would not be serviced by BMW dealers. This was particularly the case for replacement parts which could be bought from generic specialists (e.g. exhausts and brakes from Kwik-Fit). In an attempt to alter the situation, BMW dealers in the UK launched a National Fitted Price Campaign in 1994 for BMWs more than four years old. This gave a discount of forty per cent off the usual price for fitting a range of genuine BMW replacement parts including exhausts, brake pads, batteries, windshields/windscreens, clutches, and shock absorbers. The discounted prices were very competitive with those of the generic specialists. The campaign was successful in

bringing back to the dealerships many older vehicles although, as could be expected, the number of customers for more commonly replaced parts (e.g. exhausts) exceeded those for less commonly replaced parts (e.g. clutches).

Questions 9.42–9.44 relate to this case study

9.42*

The case study describes activities at which phase(s) of the service life cycle?

A decline

B maturity

C growth

D introduction

E cannot be determined

9.43*

Which of the following is **unlikely** to be an outcome of the servicing policy?

A the overall profitability of the service department will increase

B non-discounted service sales for older vehicles will increase

C the attitude of owners of older vehicles towards BMW will improve

D brand loyalty towards BMW service parts will increase

E the probability of a new service customer buying a new or used car from the dealership will increase

9.44

BMW would expect to make the bulk of its service revenue when a given model was at which phase(s) of its PLC?

A growth

B maturity

C decline

D growth and maturity

E maturity and decline

9.45

Intensive distribution is a recommended strategy at which phases of the PLC?

1 introduction

2 growth

3 maturity

4 decline

A 1 and 2

B 1 and 3

C 2 and 3

D 2 and 4

E 3 and 4

9.46

If a company is in an unattractive industry but possesses competitive strengths, an appropriate decline-phase strategy would be to:

A strengthen investment in profitable niches and cut back other investment

B maintain the company's investment level, at least for the short term

C harvest the company's investments to recover cash quickly

D increase the company's investment to strengthen its competitive position

E divest itself of the business as advantageously as possible

9.47

If a company is in an attractive industry and possesses competitive strengths, an appropriate decline-phase strategy would be to:

A strengthen investment in profitable niches and cut back other investment

B maintain the company's investment level, at least for the short term

C harvest the company's investments to recover cash quickly

D increase the company's investment to strengthen its competitive position

E divest itself of the business as advantageously as possible

9.48

As a planning tool, the PLC is well suited to:

1 characterizing the main marketing challenges in each stage

2 posing major alternative marketing strategies

3 predicting the length of each stage

4 determining where to position a product in the market

5 defining barriers to market exit

A 1 and 2

B 1 and 3

C 2 and 3

D 3 and 4

E 4 and 5

9.49

The PLC concept fails to take account of all of the following **except**:

A the changing requirements of customers

B the objectives and strategies of competitors

C the attractiveness of the market to new competitors

D the theory of diffusion and adoption of innovations

E the emergence of new technologies which can replace existing solutions

9.50

Which of the following statements appear to be **true** in relation to PLC theory?

1 management should attempt only those marketing strategies prescribed by PLC theory

2 the standard S-shaped curve used to illustrate the concept appears to describe only a minority of products

3 if a brand's sales are declining, one cannot conclude that the brand is inevitably in the decline stage

4 the concept does not allow comparisons between two similar products marketed at different times

5 the PLC is an independent variable to which companies should adapt their marketing plans

A 1 and 2

B 1 and 3

C 2 and 3

D 3 and 4

E 4 and 5

10

PRICES AND PRICING STRATEGY

10.1

Demand is likely to become more elastic under which of the following conditions?

A the customers are slow to change their buying habits

B the customers are showing greater price sensitivity

C the higher price has been concealed from the customers by a reduction in product size (e.g. a reduction in the weight of a candy bar)

D there are few or no substitutes or competitors

E the customers think the higher prices are justified

10.2

Which of the following conditions are associated with demand inelasticity?

1 the availability of many similar goods from which to choose

2 the customer is brand-loyal

3 the customer requires a life-saving drug

4 the customer has not yet decided whether to buy

5 part of the purchase is being borne by another party

A 1 and 2

B 1 and 3

C 2 and 3

D 3 and 4

E 4 and 5

10.3*

Customers tend to become more price sensitive when the product:

A is used in conjunction with a product previously bought

B can easily be compared for quality with substitutes

C is assumed to have prestige

D is unique

E cannot easily be stored

10.4

Which of the following criticisms of the demand function as it relates to consumer durables is **unjustified**?

A the price-quantity relationship depicted by the demand curve is not generally relevant for most consumer durables

B non-price factors, which are not accounted for by the concept, often exert a powerful influence on demand

C a price cut may fail to improve market share because competitors have matched it

D markets are heterogeneous, not homogeneous, and consequently are made up of not one, but a series of, demand factors

E a firm's overall pricing strategy, rather than a simple consideration of demand, will substantially influence price

10.5*

Which of the following statements **incorrectly** expresses the importance of price to marketers?

A the sales effect of a price change shows up relatively quickly, whereas variations with other marketing elements may take longer to affect sales

B in contrast to almost all other marketing measures, pricing alterations can be made without much preparatory work

C price rises tend to increase profits, whereas rises in other marketing elements tend to increase costs and therefore decrease profits

D price is the only marketing instrument use of which does not require an initially negative cash flow

E apart from the product program, price is the only marketing device that plays a major role in strategic planning concepts, especially in connection with the experience curve

10.6

Which of the following **cannot** be considered to be price variables in the marketing mix?

1 discounts
2 returns
3 warranties
4 allowances
5 inventories

A 1 and 2
B 1 and 3
C 2 and 3
D 3 and 4
E 4 and 5

10.7

If a company's aim with a new product is maximum sales growth, it should:

A cut the price to cover variable costs and some fixed costs
B set its price as low as possible to win a large market share
C set a price that makes it just worthwhile for some market segments to adopt the new product
D set a price that will maximize sales revenue
E set a price that will produce maximum cash flow

10.8*

If a company's aim with a new product is to skim the market, it should:

A cut the price to cover variable costs and some fixed costs
B set its price as low as possible to win a large market share
C set a price that makes it just worthwhile for some market segments to adopt the new product
D set a price that will maximize sales revenue
E set a price that will produce maximum cash flow

10.9

The price of a product often changes through the course of its PLC because:

1 cost reductions through the economies of scale result in lower prices
2 competitive forces may require price adjustments
3 marketing objectives usually change as the PLC progresses

4 a single price level cannot be maintained indefinitely
5 the PLC determines which pricing policy is appropriate

A 1 and 2
B 1 and 3
C 2 and 3
D 3 and 4
E 4 and 5

10.10

Which of the following price objectives is the odd one out?

A achieve a target return on investment
B maximize profits
C undercut the competition
D increase cash flow
E keep a going concern

10.11*

Sales-based pricing objectives would be **inappropriate** for a company in which of the following situations?

A the company has a limited production capacity
B one of the company's priorities is to achieve a certain return on investment
C total profit is more important to the company than per-unit profit
D the company wants to maintain market share
E the company wants to increase market share

10.12

If price is low and product quality is medium, the marketing mix reflects which strategy?

A high-value
B good-value
C economy
D superb-value
E poor-value

10.13*

If price is medium and product quality is high, the marketing mix reflects which strategy?

A high-value
B good-value
C economy

D superb-value

E poor-value

10.14*

If price is medium and product quality is low, the marketing mix reflects which strategy?

A high-value

B good-value

C economy

D superb-value

E poor-value

Case Study 10.1
The Times

In September 1993, *The Times* (with a circulation of about 370,000) cut its price from 45 pence to 30 pence in order, so *The Times* claimed, to give its readers the best possible value among British quality newspapers and to become permanently profitable for the first time in postwar years. The intention appears to have been to gain readers from the quality-market leader, *The Daily Telegraph* (whose circulation was about 1,030,000), but *The Independent* (circulation of about 270,000) also stood to lose readers. In October 1993, *The Independent* increased its daily price from 45 pence to 50 pence to coincide with an expansion of the paper, but the other quality papers held their prices. In the next eight months, *The Times'* sales steadily increased. Circulation figures for May 1994 revealed that *The Daily Telegraph* sales had slipped for the second successive month, to 993,000 copies (the lowest in forty years), while *The Times* reached a record of 518,000. On 23 June 1994, *The Daily Telegraph* decided to match *The Times*, and cut its price from 48 pence to 30 pence in an effort to regain readers. The next day, *The Times* cut its price from 30 pence to 20 pence.

The Independent responded by appealing for an investigation of *The Times'* price-cutting by the Office of Fair Trading. The complaint was that *The Times* was deliberately and illegally being sold at a loss to drive weaker competitors out of the market, and that the owners were using profits from other parts of the business to cross-subsidize the new price. *The Times*, faced with a loss of revenue on sales of about £32 million since the first cut, claimed that new advertisers had been attracted by the increased sales and that the profitability of *The Times* was 'now clearly in view'. *The Daily Telegraph*, whose price-cut would cost about £40 million in a full year, believed that its drop in profits would be limited to between £5 million to £10 million because of extra revenue, reduction in tax, and cost-cutting, and that the paper would still be very profitable.

At the start of June 1994, *The Independent* began selling selected editions outside London at 40 pence and 45 pence, while retaining the main price of 50 pence. At the start of July, i.e. after *The Times'* cut, it began selling copies at 35 pence in Birmingham. At the end of July, *The Independent* cut its price in all localities to 30 pence lest circulation should continue to deteriorate on the basis of price competition in the year or so before the Office of Fair Trading issued its report.

Questions 10.15–10.18 relate to this case study

10.15*

From the viewpoint of *The Independent*, *The Times* was employing which type of pricing?

A loss leader

B penetration

C promotional

D predatory

E dump

10.16*

From the viewpoint of *The Times*, it was employing which type of pricing?

A loss leader

B penetration

C promotional

D predatory

E dump

10.17*

From the start of June until the end of July 1994, *The Independent* was employing which type of pricing outside London?

A going rate

B test-market

C geographic

D discount

E perceived value

10.18

If *The Daily Telegraph* were to cut its price to 20 pence to again match *The Times*, it would be reasonable to expect that *The Times* would:

A retain its price

B cut its price further

C retain its price but initiate a series of promotions

D cut its price and initiate a series of promotions

E cannot be determined

10.19

Competitive reaction to a low-price market entrant is likely to be greatest when:

A the entrant is not viewed as a potentially major player in the industry

B the market is growing relatively quickly

C customers see few differences between competitors

D the industry is characterized by low fixed costs

E the entrant signals its market share objectives are modest

10.20

The strategy of some companies to initiate price cuts in a drive to dominate the market through lower costs is associated with:

A no risk

B negligible risk

C low risk

D medium risk

E high risk

10.21

Which of the following is **not** a circumstance conducive to a price-cutting decision by a firm?

A the firm has excess capacity

B the firm has been losing market share

C the industry is characterized by 'follow-the-leader' pricing

D the market is new and has not yet stabilized, and the firm wants to achieve market leadership

E the economy is going through a period of recession

10.22

A company specializing in servicing fire extinguishers canvasses a relatively small town where a rival, who has been established for some years, has signed up most of the businesses. The new company promises shop-keepers that it will service and re-charge up to three appliances annually for a total of £16 instead of the current contractor's price of £22. Which of the following outcomes is **least** likely?

A potential customers will ask the existing contractor to match the lower price

B if the customer switches to the new company, the former contractor will permanently lose market share in that town

C potential customers may assume that the quality of the low-price service will not be as good as they have been receiving

D the existing contractor will at least match the new price until the threat is over

E all the outcomes are equally as likely

10.23*

Which of the following statements **incorrectly** depicts the strategic implications of a price war?

A if price is the sole basis of competition, competitors can take away the competitive advantage relatively easily

B companies with relatively small cash reserves are ill-advised to enter into a price war

C industries characterized by product differentiation based solely on quality are less likely to be affected by price wars

D price wars tend to reduce or destroy the incentive to invest in an industry

E the greater a company's cost advantage, the more likely it is to make a success of price competition

Case Study 10.2
ABC Ltd

ABC Ltd is considering which of several pricing strategies to implement. Market research has been done to find the expected outcome of each strategy (see Table 10.1). The company's income statement is presented in Table 10.2.

Questions 10.24–10.26 relate to this case study

Table 10.1
Expected outcomes of ABC Ltd's alternative pricing strategies

Strategy	Expected outcome on sales volume
1: cut price by 5%	no effect
2: cut price by 10%	10% increase
3: cut price by 20%	40% increase
4: increase price by 5%	2% decrease
5: increase price by 10%	15% decrease

Table 10.2
ABC Ltd income statement

		£million
Sales (10,000 units)		100
Variable costs		
Discounts and allowances	15	
Materials	15	
Direct labour	20	
Other variable costs	10	60
Contribution		40
Fixed overheads		
Marketing	5	
Research and development	5	
Other fixed costs	20	30
Net profit		10

10.24*

Which pricing strategy could be expected to have the **most** beneficial effect on ABC's profits?

A strategy 1
B strategy 2
C strategy 3
D strategy 4
E strategy 5

10.25*

Which pricing strategy could be expected to have the **least** beneficial effect on ABC's profits?

A strategy 1
B strategy 2
C strategy 3
D strategy 4
E strategy 5

10.26

Which would be the most appropriate motive for following strategy 1?

A to gain newspaper publicity
B to try to protect market share in a period of price competition
C to increase the number of times the inventory turns over in a year
D to initiate a price war
E to encourage a take-over bid for the business

10.27

Which of the following techniques is **unlikely** to reduce customers' sensitivity to price increases?

A product unbundling
B line extensions
C multiple-unit pricing
D brand repositioning
E none of these

10.28

A major manufacturer of unbranded goods increases its prices to the trade twice a year, in January and July. A retailer who buys a large proportion of stock from this supplier would be well-advised **not** to:

A try to minimize the frequency of price increases
B raise prices to take into account both the current increase in costs and the increase anticipated in six months
C take into account the reaction of the main target customers when deciding on the level of price increases
D try to reduce prices of some other goods when the prices of the major manufacturer's goods increase
E raise prices when everyone else does

10.29

Which of the following factors tend to desensitize customers to more modest price rises?

1 legal requirements to display prices
2 prominent in-store displays
3 consumer loyalty to products or stores
4 the effects of product differentiation
5 television advertising

A 1 and 2
B 1 and 3
C 2 and 3
D 3 and 4
E 4 and 5

10.30

Which of the following pricing methods represent a cost-orientated approach?

1 going-rate pricing
2 psychological pricing
3 target-return pricing
4 markup pricing
5 sealed-bid pricing

A 1 and 2

B 1 and 3

C 2 and 3

D 3 and 4

E 4 and 5

10.31

Which of the following statements **incorrectly** characterizes perceived-value pricing?

A non-price variables in the marketing mix are very important in building up perceived value in the customer's mind

B the seller's costs are not taken into account when perceived-value pricing is used in product planning

C perceived-value pricing is more sensitive to consumer demand than is cost-based pricing

D perceived value pricing is based on customers' trade-offs between one product's expected benefits and its price relative to those of competing products

E perceived-value pricing complements product-positioning thinking

10.32

Which of the following statements **incorrectly** criticizes cost-based methods of pricing?

A they inadequately reflect competition

B they assume that all products should absorb the fixed expenses of the business at the same rate

C the concept of profit as an addition to unit costs is a false one

D they ignore demand

E complexity in applying the various formulae makes it difficult to derive cost-based prices

10.33

Public utilities such as gas or electricity tend to use which form of pricing?

A going-rate pricing

B price-floor pricing

C cost-plus pricing

D target-return pricing

E markup pricing

10.34

Wholesalers tend to use which form of pricing?

A going-rate pricing

B price-floor pricing

C cost-plus pricing

D target-return pricing

E markup pricing

10.35*

In a certain city, the average price for one ounce of imported perfume is £20. A manufacturer who recommends selling one ounce of a well-known brand of perfume (costing the retailer £10) for £50 is engaging in which of the following pricing strategies?

1 psychological pricing

2 cost-plus pricing

3 price-quality pricing

4 special event pricing

5 geographical pricing

A 1 and 2

B 1 and 3

C 2 and 3

D 3 and 4

E 4 and 5

10.36*

A theatre charges £33.50 for orchestra/stall seats and £16.75 for balcony seats for evening performances, but £16.75 and £10.00, respectively, for the same seats at matinees. Which of the following pricing tactics is the theatre using?

1 customer-segment pricing

2 location pricing

3 time pricing

4 image pricing

5 product-form pricing

A 1 and 2

B 1 and 3

C 2 and 3

D 3 and 4

E 4 and 5

10.37

A pizza restaurant normally charges £11.99 for an 18-inch 'New York style' cheese and tomato pizza, and £12.99 for the same pizza with the addition of mushrooms, peppers, olives, or extra cheese. Students are given £1.50 off the purchase of these pizzas before 7 p.m. from Sunday to Thursday. Which of the following pricing tactics is the restaurant using?

1 time pricing

2 location pricing

3 image pricing

4 customer-segment pricing

5 product-form pricing

A 1 and 2

B 1 and 3

C 2 and 3

D 3 and 4

E 4 and 5

10.38*

A retailer who wants to use a well-conceived product-line pricing strategy to sell men's shirts may be advised to use which of the following sets of price points?

1 £10, £18, £20

2 £10, £12, £20

3 £10, £12, £14, £16, £18, £20

4 £10, £15, £20

5 £10, £20

A 1 and 2

B 1 and 3

C 2 and 3

D 3 and 4

E 4 and 5

10.39*

A furniture company offers three models of the same coffee table: in oak finish for £110, in oak veneer for £190, and in solid oak for £300. The company is using:

A captive-product pricing

B optional-feature pricing

C leader (or leading-line) pricing

D premium pricing

E product-bundling pricing

10.40

At the end of 1993, B & Q, a large do-it-yourself retailer trading from warehouses, began offering 'low prices when you want them – that's every day' on the 500 products most regularly bought by B & Q customers. The company was using:

A captive-product pricing

B optional-feature pricing

C leader (or leading-line) pricing

D premium pricing

E product-bundling pricing

10.41

In the summer of 1994, Kentucky Fried Chicken restaurants offered a 'KFC Family Dinner', consisting of eight pieces of chicken, four portions of French fried potatoes, a large coleslaw, baked beans, and a family size Sarah Lee apple pie, for £9.99. This is an example of:

A captive-product pricing

B optional-feature pricing

C leader (or leading-line) pricing

D premium pricing

E product-bundling pricing

10.42

In price negotiations, sellers are in a strong position over buyers in the following situations **except** when:

A the buyer purchases small quantities

B the cost of the item is a small part of the buyer's costs

C buyers have a relatively low quality image

D the cost of the product failing would be high

E sellers are in a strong position over buyers in all of these situations

Case Study 10.3
Sainsbury's Classic Cola

In mid-April 1994, Britain's largest supermarket chain, Sainsbury's, introduced 'original American taste' Sainsbury's Classic Cola, in competition to Coca-Cola, the market leader in colas. Little advertising accompanied the introduction. However, there was a good deal of publicity because Coca-Cola accused Sainsburys of copying its packaging, if not product taste (Classic Coca-Cola is not sold in Britain, so there was no protest at Sainsbury's choice of product name). On launch, Sainsbury's cola was priced at 59 pence for a two litre bottle, against £1.05 for Coca-Cola. About one month after launch, the price of Sainsbury's cola rose to 69 pence for two litres. During the same period, Sainsbury's sold other own-brand carbonated soft-drinks for as little as 49 pence for two litres.

Because of pressure from Coca-Cola, Sainsbury's slightly amended its package graphics a few weeks after launch. Coca-Cola also changed the package graphics on some of its products. After two months, Sainsbury's Classic Cola accounted for 68 per cent of all cola sales at Sainsbury's (up from 13 per cent for its previous own-brand cola), and 15 per cent of all cola sales in the United

Kingdom. Coca-Cola's sales at Sainsbury's fell to 22 per cent (down from 66 per cent). Meanwhile, Pepsi's share of cola sales at Sainsbury's dropped from 20 per cent to less than 9 per cent. Helped by a warm summer and the publicity given to the 'cola war', the cola market grew by more than 20 per cent by the end of June, and the sale of Coke was in fact higher than it was before the launch of Classic.

Questions 10.43–10.45 relate to this case study

10.43*

The initial 59 pence price for two litres of Sainsbury's Classic Cola was a:

A loss leader price

B baseline price

C discount price

D customary price

E promotion price

10.44

In a 'summer special' at the end of July, Sainsbury's cut the price of a 330 ml can of Classic Cola to 17 pence when purchasing a 24-can pack at £3.99 Standard 8-can Classic packs continued to sell for an average of 21 pence per can (8 cans for £1.69), and a can of Coke could be bought at Sainsbury's for 20 pence if two 8-can packs were bought for £3.28. The price of 17 pence per can of Classic Cola was a:

A loss leader price

B baseline price

C discount price

D customary price

E promotion price

10.45

Sainsbury's strategy in competition with Coca-Cola appears to have focused on:

A encouraging customers to re-evaluate brands

B employing bait-and-switch pricing

C buying market share

D emphasizing the price-quality relationship

E developing a better product

10.46*

Which of the following characteristics are **not** normally associated with defensive pricing?

1 it maximizes short-term profits

2 it enhances a product's quality image

3 its application is usually confined to a few commodity groups

4 it may follow specific penetration activities by a competitor

5 it leads to market stabilization

A 1 and 2

B 1 and 3

C 2 and 3

D 3 and 4

E 4 and 5

10.47

Several shops in a town sell broadly comparable (but not usually identical) merchandise. One retailer, in determining where to price-position her shop, knows that she offers a higher level of service, a wider selection of goods, a nicer-looking shop, and a better location than her competitors. Which of the following strategies is she well-advised to adopt?

A price with the competition

B price below the competition

C price above the competition

D price above the competition, but then reduce prices to be with the competition

E price below the competition, but then raise prices to be with the competition

10.48*

During periods of rapidly rising costs, which of the following strategies would be **least** advisable, from a marketing viewpoint, for a manufacturer to follow?

A leave products unchanged, and pass along all of the cost increases to customers

B leave products unchanged, and pass along only part of the cost increases to customers

C modify products to hold down costs (e.g. by offering fewer options or reducing quality), and maintain prices

D modify products to gain consumer support for higher prices (e.g. by offering more options or increasing quality)

E cannot be determined

10.49*

In a period of economic recession, which of the following pricing policies would be most likely to result in maintenance of both market share and long-term profitability?

A cut price fully, and reduce perceived value

B cut price partly, and raise perceived value

C maintain price, and reduce perceived value

D maintain both price and perceived value

E maintain price, and raise perceived value

10.50*

Non-price competition would normally be attractive for manufacturers in the following situations **except** when:

A most manufacturers produce a product that is virtually indistinguishable from the competition

B the industry is characterized by a state of oligopoly

C the market can be divided into several viable segments

D there are many manufacturers in the industry

E demand for the product is inelastic

11

MARKETING CHANNELS AND PHYSICAL DISTRIBUTION

11.1
Which of the following is the odd one out?

A retailing

B logistics

C customer support

D purchasing

E budgeting

11.2
In considering the relationship between various consumer product classes and ideal distribution objectives, a marketer should first take into account:

A the price of the product

B the cost of distribution alternatives

C the target market's view of the product

D the manufacturer's view of the product

E the retailer's view of the product

11.3
For a single product, the type and number of distribution arrangements required should depend on:

1 any differences between market segments interested in the product

2 the product's progress in relation to the product life cycle

3 the number of market segments interested in the product

4 the distribution arrangements used by competitors for similar products

5 the uses to which the product may be put

A 1 and 2

B 1 and 3

C 2 and 3

D 3 and 4

E 4 and 5

11.4*
The physical-distribution objective of getting the right goods to the right places at the right time for the least cost is:

A appropriate for industrial goods, but not for consumer goods

B achievable by relatively large companies, but not relatively small companies

C possible only when the manufacturer directly controls the channels of distribution

D invalid because of the implicit trade-offs

E none of these

11.5*
Decisions on channel choice are:

A harder to change than those on product and promotion, but easier to change than those on price

B harder to change than those on promotion and price, but easier to change than those on product

C harder to change than those on price, but easier to change than those on product and promotion

D harder to change than those on product and price, but easier to change than those on promotion

E harder to change than those on product, price, and promotion

11.6
In terms of distribution, the strategic importance of a manufacturer obtaining a high national market share is that:

A supply creates demand

B retailers' decisions on whether to stock a brand are often influenced by the brand's national market share

C per-unit distribution costs for high-share brands are lower than those for low-share brands

D the higher the market share, the more space the brand will occupy on a retailer's shelf

E national market share is a better measure of a brand's distribution efficiency than is local or regional market share

11.7
The difference between merchant middlemen and agent middlemen is that:

A merchant middlemen assist in the performance of distribution without taking title to the goods or negotiating purchases or sales, whereas agent middlemen search for customers and negotiate on behalf of the producer without taking title to the goods

B merchant middlemen buy and resell merchandise without taking title to the goods, whereas agent middlemen buy and resell merchandise and take title to the goods

C merchant middlemen buy and resell merchandise and take title to the goods, whereas agent middlemen search for customers and negotiate on behalf of the producer without taking title to the goods

D merchant middlemen search for customers and negotiate on behalf of the producer without taking title to the goods, whereas agent middlemen search for customers and negotiate on behalf of the producer and take title to the goods

E merchant middlemen buy and resell merchandise and take title to the goods, whereas agent middlemen assist in the performance of distribution without taking title to the goods or negotiating purchases or sales

11.8*
All of the following are termed marketing intermediary facilitators **except**:

1 brokers
2 advertising agencies
3 retailers
4 banks
5 transportation companies

A 1 and 2
B 1 and 3
C 2 and 3
D 3 and 4
E 4 and 5

11.9
Which of the following is **not** an advantage of using a marketing intermediary?

A marketing intermediaries lessen a producer's risk of product failure

B producers lacking sufficient financial resources can be helped by the use of marketing intermediaries

C marketing intermediaries allow specialist producers to find outlets for their goods without having to diversify their businesses

D producers may be able to achieve a higher rate of return on investment by concentrating on their main business

E using marketing intermediaries often allows producers to achieve savings in distribution

11.10
The role of marketing channels is to:

A maximize producers' profits

B bridge the discrepancy between the assortment of goods generated by the producer and the assortment demanded by the consumer

C create demand for producers' products

D smooth the flow of all goods and services

E all of the above

11.11*
Which of the following represents a backward marketing-channel flow?

A promotion

B ordering

C physical possession

D collection and dissemination of marketing research information

E none of these

11.12
If a manufacturer assumes the marketing functions performed by wholesalers, the functions are said to have been:

A eliminated from the channel

B shifted backward in the channel

C shifted downward in the channel

D shifted forward in the channel

E shifted upward in the channel

11.13*
Which of the following industries exemplifies a backward channel of distribution?

A radio-controlled taxis

B waste paper recycling

C sporting goods

D self-assembly furniture

E electricity supply

11.14*

Which is the odd one out in terms of channels of distribution?

A corner grocery shop

B door-to-door sales

C home party selling

D mail order sales

E manufacturer-owned store

11.15*

In a traditional/conventional channel system:

A the objectives of the various channel members are the same

B control is usually maintained by the producer

C direct marketing is more important than indirect marketing

D the various channel members limit their relations to buying from and selling to each other

E there may be backward integration, but not forward integration

11.16

Which of the following **incorrectly** characterizes a traditional/conventional channel system?

A each channel member seeks to maximize its own profits

B the network is highly fragmented

C the members bargain with each other at arm's length

D the channel is professionally managed

E none of these

11.17

Industrial marketing may make use of the following channels **except**:

A zero-level channels

B one-level channels

C two-level channels

D dual channels

E all may be used

11.18

The channel system likely to cause most conflict between the middlemen and the producer is:

A zero-level channels

B one-level channels

C two-level channels

D dual channels

E three-level channels

11.19

Which of the following is **not** part of the procedure for designing a channel system?

A analyzing customer needs

B identifying the major channel alternatives

C establishing channel objectives

D evaluating the major channel alternatives

E selecting channel members

11.20

Cost-benefit analysis of a distribution system would **not** normally include:

A identifying the dimensions of service that customers value

B determining the cost of guaranteeing a 100 per cent in-stock position

C estimating the revenue effect of changes in service levels

D weighting the service dimensions by importance

E estimating the costs of providing different levels of service

11.21

Which of the following is **not** a dimension of service in distribution?

A minimum order size

B waiting time

C assortment breadth

D stock availability

E delivery charges

11.22*

Which of the following factors normally favour the choice of long channels?

1 the customers are geographically concentrated

2 the company is new to the market

3 the economy is going through a recession

4 the product is relatively heavy

5 the product is technically complex

A 1 and 2

B 1 and 3

C 2 and 3

D 3 and 4

E 4 and 5

11.23*

Which of the following factors normally favour the choice of short channels?

1 there are few customers

2 no installation or servicing assistance is required

3 managerial capabilities are weak

4 the market to be served is old

5 the value of the product is high

A 1 and 2

B 1 and 3

C 2 and 3

D 3 and 4

E 4 and 5

11.24

The types of products most likely to benefit from exclusive distribution are:

1 furniture

2 office supplies

3 new cars

4 designer clothes

5 household products

A 1 and 2

B 1 and 3

C 2 and 3

D 3 and 4

E 4 and 5

11.25*

In which of these situations would a selective distribution strategy be advisable?

A the consumer prefers to buy the most readily available brand of product at the most accessible store

B the consumer is indifferent to the brand of product bought but shops at different stores to secure a better price

C the consumer has a preference for a specific store because of the brands it carries

D the consumer is indifferent to the brand of product bought but shops at different stores to secure better retail service

E the consumer selects a purchase from among the assortment carried by the most accessible store

11.26*

In which of these situations would an intensive distribution strategy be advisable?

A the consumer makes comparisons among both retail-controlled factors and factors associated with the product or brand

B the consumer selects a purchase from among the most accessible stores carrying the item in stock

C the consumer has a strong preference regarding product brand but shops at a number of stores to secure the best price for this brand

D the consumer prefers to shop at a certain store, but is indifferent to the brand of product purchased

E the consumer prefers to shop at a certain store but is uncertain as to which product to buy and examines the store's stock for the best purchase

11.27

An undifferentiated marketing strategy is complemented by which of the following distribution strategies?

A selective

B intensive

C exclusive

D intensive or selective

E selective or exclusive

11.28

A differentiated marketing strategy is complemented by which of the following distribution strategies?

A selective

B intensive

C exclusive

D intensive or selective

E selective or exclusive

11.29

A concentrated marketing strategy is complemented by which of the following distribution strategies?

A selective

B intensive

C exclusive

D intensive or selective

E selective or exclusive

11.30

A raid penetration strategy is complemented by which of the following distribution strategies?

A selective

B intensive

C exclusive

D intensive or selective

E selective or exclusive

11.31

According to product life cycle (PLC) theory, building intensive distribution is the appropriate strategy for which phases?

1 introduction

2 growth

3 maturity

4 decline

A 1 and 2

B 2 and 3

C 2 and 4

D 3 and 4

E none of these combinations

11.32

According to product life cycle (PLC) theory, selective distribution is preferable for which phases?

1 introduction

2 growth

3 maturity

4 decline

A 1 and 2

B 2 and 3

C 2 and 4

D 3 and 4

E none of these combinations

11.33

Which of the following criteria is **not** usually considered by producers in evaluating channel alternatives?

A sales and costs

B reputation of channel members

C duration and flexibility of commitment

D channel capabilities

E degree of control over the channel

11.34

A company (direct) salesforce is preferable to a manufacturers' sales agency when:

1 the company wants to avoid a high fixed-cost operation

2 the company has very few products to sell

3 the company cannot commit a high level of resources

4 special training is required to demonstrate and sell the product

5 a business is willing to sacrifice short-term profit for the sake of ambitious long-term market share goals

A 1 and 2

B 1 and 3

C 2 and 3

D 3 and 4

E 4 and 5

11.35

Which of the following **incorrectly** characterizes a vertical marketing system?

A members of the channel act in a unified way

B any one channel member owns the others, controls them, or has the power to make them co-operate

C emphasis is on achieving operating economies and maximum market impact

D VMSs are less stable than traditional/conventional channels

E VMSs can be dominated by a producer, wholesaler, or retailer

11.36

A franchise system (such as Burger King in fast foods or Avis in car rentals) is an example of the:

A administered VMS

B corporate VMS

C contractual VMS

D traditional/conventional marketing system

E horizontal marketing system

11.37*

A door manufacturer sells part of its output to whole-salers dealing with retailers, and the rest to builders' merchants dealing with contractors and retailers. This is an example of the:

A administered VMS

B corporate VMS

C contractual VMS

D traditional/conventional marketing system

E horizontal marketing system

11.38

California's Gallo wine company makes wine from its own vineyards, manufactures the bottles and screw caps, and owns its own trucks to distribute to many of its important markets. This is an example of the:

A administered VMS

B corporate VMS

C contractual VMS

D traditional/conventional marketing system

E horizontal marketing system

11.39

A perfume concession in a department store is an exam-ple of the:

A administered VMS

B corporate VMS

C contractual VMS

D traditional/conventional marketing system

E horizontal marketing system

11.40*

BT is the UK's largest company and one of the world's leading suppliers of international telecommunications. MCI is the second largest long-distance telecom-munications carrier in the US, and internationally one of the world's fastest growing. In mid-1994, they pooled $1 billion in resources to form Concert, one of the first companies dedicated to creating a fully integrated global telecommunications network. Concert is an example of the:

A administered VMS

B corporate VMS

C contractual VMS

D traditional/conventional marketing system

E horizontal marketing system

11.41*

A market leader is launching a new range of products and wants to insure that all of its customers carry it and give its introduction some prominence. Against a back-ground of its own programme of national and region-al advertising, the manufacturer is giving retailers special discounts for initial orders and is providing them with display materials. The manufacturer is also offer-ing rebates to cover part of the cost of retailer-spon-sored advertising of the range. Which marketing system is being employed?

A administered VMS

B corporate VMS

C contractual VMS

D traditional/conventional marketing system

E horizontal marketing system

11.42

We would expect to find the greatest amount of chan-nel co-operation with the:

A administered VMS

B corporate VMS

C contractual VMS

D traditional/conventional marketing system

E horizontal marketing system

11.43

A push strategy for a producer may entail which of the following tactics?

1 supplying the intermediary with merchandise on a sale-or-return basis

2 issuing coupons or free samples

3 offering the intermediary a promotional discount

4 periodic sales visits involving stock adjustments as well as order-taking

5 heavy and prolonged television advertising

A 1 and 2

B 1 and 3

C 2 and 3

D 3 and 4

E 4 and 5

11.44

A pull strategy for a producer will usually be most effec-tive when:

1 the product is innovative and is just being intro-duced

2 the various channel members want to co-operate in the marketing efforts for the product

3 the demand for the product is growing rapidly

4 many products are already competing in all desired outlets

5 the firm is new to the market and is trying to break into an existing channel

A 1 and 2

B 1 and 3

C 2 and 3

D 3 and 4

E 4 and 5

11.45

All of the following are physical distribution functions of intermediaries **except**:

A transferring ownership/title of a product

B breaking bulk

C accumulating bulk

D creating assortments

E reducing the number of transactions necessary to accomplish the exchange of a product

11.46

Which of the following would **not** be an advantage of using a third party distribution company?

A stock rotation/product control is increased

B the amount of capital employed in distribution is limited

C operating costs, both overall and in peripheral areas, are lower

D geographical coverage is expanded

E overall risk is reduced

11.47*

Which of the following customer service elements of the physical distribution function is the odd one out?

A written statements of service policy

B product availability

C order cycle time

D delivery reliability

E order status information

11.48

The main reason that some manufacturers impose a standard delivery charge on orders under a certain value, but deliver orders over that value free-of-charge, is that:

A customer demand is not tied to inventory levels

B fixed distribution costs are higher for small orders than for large

C these manufacturers want to encourage only large orders

D costs for small orders are high compared with the value of shipments

E modern warehouses are inefficient for small orders

11.49*

A firm's re-order point for each of its products, raw materials, or parts usually depends on the:

A availability of quantity discounts, the costs of processing each order, and the costs of maintaining goods in inventory

B annual sales (or usage) in units, the costs of processing each order, the cost of each unit, and the carrying costs as a percentage of cost

C order lead time, the usage rate, and safety stock

D cost of each unit, costs of processing each order, the usage rate, and the costs of maintaining goods in inventory

E none of these

11.50*

Which of the following are **not** usually characteristics of a just-in-time (JIT) inventory system?

1 very rapid changes in production-run planning

2 wider product ranges

3 long production runs

4 deliveries of components in small lots

5 a sophisticated management information system

A 1 and 2

B 1 and 3

C 2 and 3

D 3 and 4

E 4 and 5

12

RETAILING

12.1
The first step in strategic retail planning should be:

A segmenting the market

B finding a suitable premises

C assessing the availability of a suitable workforce

D analysing the nature of the business opportunity

E insuring that sufficient finance is available

12.2
A suitable market-oriented mission for a corner grocery shop might be:

A to sell the most popular fruit and vegetables

B to offer convenience

C to sell hard-to-find products

D to be the most up-to-date grocery shop in the area

E to make a net profit of 4 to 6 per cent of turnover

12.3
If a retailer finds that sales consistently fail to achieve forecasts, the best course of action is to:

A replace some or all of the sales assistants

B revise the forecasts downwards

C embark on a strategy of hyper-segmentation

D reassess the bases of the forecasts

E institute an incentives scheme for the staff

12.4*
Those who use the theory of natural selection, or survival of the fittest, in the assessment of the survival and growth of retail institutions:

A will be able to predict correctly about 60 per cent of the time

B will be able to predict correctly about 80 per cent of the time

C will be unable to predict which qualities will be most valuable

D will be unable to apply the theory to other institutions

E have been unable to defend this Darwinian theory in the face of the 'Big Bang' theory of retail development

12.5
Which of the following concepts are **inappropriate** to the wheel of retailing theory?

1 analysis of overheads

2 analysis of price levels

3 analysis of management structure

4 analysis of store location

5 analysis of service offerings

A 1 and 2

B 1 and 3

C 2 and 3

D 3 and 4

E 4 and 5

12.6*
Which of the following concepts does the accordion theory share with the theory of natural selection and the wheel of retailing theory?

1 degree of merchandise balance

2 size of retail establishment

3 importance of cost management

4 simplification of marketing channels

5 emphasis on merchandise handling

A 1 and 2

B 1 and 3

C 2 and 3

D 3 and 4

E 4 and 5

12.7*
A specialty shop selling only clothing can be classified as a:

A single-line shop

B limited-line shop

C broad-line shop

D selective-line shop

E super-specialty shop

12.8

In food retailing, the type of shop characterized by narrow product assortment and high price would be a:

A combination shop

B supermarket

C superstore

D hypermarket

E convenience store

12.9

In which of the following types of shops would we expect to find shopping goods?

1 self-service

2 self-selection

3 limited service

4 full-service

A 1 and 2

B 1 and 3

C 2 and 3

D 2 and 4

E 3 and 4

Case Study 12.1
Men's wool overcoats

Three particular men's shops in central London sell pure wool overcoats. Shop A carries only the Burberry brand (ranging in price from £495 to £575); shop B, only the Crombie brand (from £375 to £395); and shop C, two unfamiliar brands (from £150 to £195). An 'average price' wool overcoat was selling for around £150 at the time.

Questions 12.10–12.11 relate to this case study

12.10*

In a comparison of shop A with shop B, it appears that:

1 the shops have selected different target markets

2 the shops are engaging in price competition

3 the shops have attempted enterprise differentiation

4 the shops are engaging in non-price competition

5 the shops have different service levels

A 1 and 2

B 1 and 3

C 2 and 3

D 3 and 4

E 4 and 5

12.11*

In a comparison of shop A with shop C, it appears that:

1 the shops have selected different target markets

2 the shops are engaging in price competition

3 the shops have attempted enterprise differentiation

4 the shops are engaging in non-price competition

5 the shops have different service levels

A 1 and 2

B 1 and 3

C 2 and 3

D 3 and 4

E 4 and 5

12.12

Which of the following retailers are involved in intra-type competition?

1 Comet electrical appliance warehouse

2 Harrods department store

3 Selfridges department store

4 Woolworths variety store

5 Allied Carpets superstore

A 1 and 2

B 1 and 3

C 2 and 3

D 3 and 4

E 4 and 5

12.13

Which of the following retailers are involved in inter-type competition?

1 Sainsburys supermarket

2 Argos catalogue showroom

3 Marks & Spencers clothing, household soft goods, and food store

4 BhS clothing, household soft goods, and lighting store

5 Halfords automotive accessory shop

A 1 and 2

B 1 and 3

C 2 and 3

D 3 and 4

E 4 and 5

12.14*

For which of the following elements of the retail marketing mix does the owner of a shop under franchise normally determine policy?

A product quality

B staff training

C product assortment

D suppliers

E none of these

Case Study 12.2:
Gorgeous ladieswear

Gorgeous, a ladieswear retailer, sells dresses (day dresses, cocktail dresses, and some evening wear), track suits, separates (blouses, jumpers, skirts, trousers, and culottes), and some coats. The goods are basically in five British fittings, from size 10 (32-inch bust/small) to size 18 (40-inch bust/extra large), and are priced for the middle of the market. For dresses, there are usually seven or eight styles in each size, and as many as three colours for each style. For track suits, there are usually six styles in each size, and as many as three colours. For separates, there are from two to six styles in each size, and up to five colours. There are three styles of coats, each in two colours, in each size.

Questions 12.15–12.22 relate to this case study

12.15*

How many product assortments does this retailer have?

A 1

B 4

C 10

D cannot be determined from the information

E none of these

12.16

How many merchandise lines does this retailer have?

A 1

B 4

C 10

D cannot be determined from the information

E none of these

12.17

If this retailer wanted to broaden the merchandise mix, a possibility would be to:

A carry size 20 in all garments

B increase the number of colours

C carry underwear

D carry cheaper goods

E inaugurate a Christmas club

12.18

If this retailer wanted to attempt a two-way stretch, the shop should:

A carry only downmarket and midmarket goods

B carry downmarket, midmarket, and upmarket goods

C carry only midmarket and upmarket goods

D carry only downmarket and upmarket goods

E carry only upmarket goods

12.19

In determining which products to buy, which of the following considerations is the shop's buyer best advised to disregard?

A anticipated profit margins

B personal preference in colours

C brand

D trade press fashion predictions

E none of these

12.20*

Larger size track suits had sold well in the past, so the buyer was surprised to find considerable unsold stocks of sizes 16 and 18 for three styles, especially since larger sizes sold as expected for the other styles of the track suits. The most probable reason for this situation is that:

A the shop's market segmentation strategy is wrong

B there was something wrong with the styles in question

C the differences in sales happened by chance

D the larger size market has reached saturation

E the poor selling styles were not given enough display prominence

12.21

If a shop's buyer mistakenly accepts a new product, the consequence is:

A usually negligible

B likely to cause only minor losses

C sometimes marked by the loss of customer goodwill

D likely to lead to a string of bad buying decisions

E likely to cause significant losses

12.22*

If a shop's buyer mistakenly retains an old product, the consequence is:

A usually negligible

B likely to cause only minor losses

C sometimes marked by the loss of customer goodwill

D likely to lead to a string of bad buying decisions

E likely to cause significant losses

12.23

Which of the following features are **not** normally associated with defensive pricing?

1 it maximizes short-term profits

2 it enhances a product's quality image

3 its application is usually confined to a few commodity groups

4 it may follow sporadic penetration activities by a competitor

5 it leads to market stabilization

A 1 and 2

B 1 and 3

C 2 and 3

D 3 and 4

E 4 and 5

12.24*

Which of the following benefits are obtained by marking down an item early in the selling season?

1 sales will have a more even pattern than with late markdowns

2 early markdowns enable a buyer to reorder the item before the season ends

3 early markdowns generally require a smaller markdown than would be needed later to get the same result

4 the image of a prestige shop is enhanced by early markdowns

5 early markdowns tend to speed stock turnover

A 1 and 2

B 1 and 3

C 2 and 3

D 3 and 4

E 4 and 5

12.25

A furniture shop usually sells three-piece suites from £499 upwards. It purchases two units of a 'basic model' suite, similar in appearance to the £499 model, and advertises them prominently in the local newspaper, stating that 'the displayed model costs only £299'. This is an example of:

A bait and switch pricing

B flexible pricing

C perceived value pricing

D multiple pricing

E loss leader pricing

12.26*

A supermarket accepts an offer whereby a manufacturer will reimburse 40 per cent of a 50 pence off price deal, and finds that the markdown causes noticeable brand switching in the product category. Which consequences could we expect to result?

1 the supermarket will delete the brand that has lost the most market share

2 there is a good chance that the offer will have a negative effect on shop profits

3 the change in consumer choice is unlikely to be permanent

4 there is a good chance that the offer will have a positive effect on shop profits

5 other manufacturers will try to match the offer

A 1 and 2

B 1 and 3

C 2 and 3

D 3 and 4

E 4 and 5

12.27

A baker selling cakes at between £1.25 and £2.50 asked consumers to taste two cakes identical in all respects except for price. Cake A was priced at £1.45, and cake B at £1.85 He found that almost 57 per cent of the sample thought cake B tasted better. On the basis of this, his best course of action is to:

A sell the cake at £1.85 and develop another cake to sell at £1.45

B sell the cake at £1.85 and not develop a cake to sell at £1.45

C test buying intention for cakes A and B before deciding on pricing

D test whether the phenomenon observed in the taste-tests is repeated for a different set of prices (e.g. £1.85 and £2.25) before deciding on pricing

E develop a different cake priced at £1.85 and test it against cake B before deciding on adoption

12.28

Most supermarket chains are offered in excess of 800 manufacturer-sponsored promotions each month, and typically feature a maximum of 60 to 70 such items at any one time. From an individual chain's point of view, the best strategy is to:

A compete directly with rivals on all the same promotional items

B compete directly with rivals on about half of the same promotional items

C avoid direct competition on the same promotional items

D refrain from carrying promotional items

E undertake promotions only for slow-selling lines

12.29*

Which of the following statements **incorrectly** characterizes leader line pricing?

A leader line prices are usually not cut as deeply as in the case of short-term offers

B there are usually fewer items involved than with short-term offers

C the selected discounted prices are held long term

D leader line pricing differs substantially from loss leader pricing

E leader line pricing may be complemented by the selective use of short-term offers

12.30

Leader line pricing is most likely to be found where a retailer:

A is a niche marketer

B has not segmented the market

C has little competition

D previously applied the same markup to every item in a range

E hopes to convey a better price image

12.31*

It was found that a certain jacket was selling for £69 in a department store's city-centre branch, and for £89 in the department store's branch in a large out-of-town shopping centre about 10 miles away. The most likely explanation of this is that:

A transport costs differed

B the city-centre shop was in a more competitive environment

C each shop targeted a different market segment

D the shops operated under different price strata within the company

E there was an error in one store's pricing

12.32

Which of the following cues would tend to signal low price levels to a consumer?

1 heavy advertising

2 wide assortment

3 free delivery service

4 late night shopping

5 fluorescent-coloured signage

A 1 and 2

B 1 and 3

C 2 and 3

D 3 and 4

E 4 and 5

12.33*

A retailer decides that a certain item should have a markup of 40 per cent on selling price. The item costs £12.00. Assuming that no additional taxes or charges are payable, the selling price of the item should be:

A £4.80

B £16.80

C £20.00

D £48.00

E none of these

12.34

A retailer promises to match a competitor's prices on identical goods if a competitor charges less, and finds that a narrow-range discounter's pricing policy is now noticeably eroding her shop's profit margins. Her best remedy is to:

A try to avoid duplication of the discounter's goods

B reduce all prices to the discounter's level

C emphasize non-price benefits of shopping at her shop in her advertising

D try to undercut the discounter on selected high-profile items

E exert what pressure she can on the manufacturers not to supply the discounter

12.35

A neighbourhood shopping centre differs from a ribbon (string street) shopping situation in that:

A customers usually drive to the former but not to the latter

B the rents per square foot are usually lower for the former than for the latter

C the former may include a supermarket, but the latter usually would not

D the former usually concentrates on shopping goods, whereas the latter usually concentrates on convenience goods

E the former is planned in advance, whereas the latter is not

12.36

In the decision to select a particular site for a shop, which of the following considerations is likely to be the **least** important?

A the history of previous businesses on the site

B traffic flow

C parking

D nearness to public transport

E nearby vacant shops and buildings

12.37*

At the end of July, following a sale, where would retailing theory indicate that a general clothing retailer should display ladies' swimsuits?

A next to a cash register

B perhaps in the window, but not on general display in the shop

C in the front third of the shop

D in the middle third of the shop

E in the back third of the shop

12.38

At the end of July, following a sale, where would retailing theory indicate that a general clothing retailer should display back-to-school clothes?

A next to a cash register

B perhaps in the window, but not on general display in the shop

C in the front third of the shop

D in the middle third of the shop

E in the back third of the shop

12.39*

In a supermarket, the best place to display bulky goods would be:

A at the end of an aisle

B near the checkout

C as low as possible on a gondola display

D close to the middle shelf on a gondola display

E as high as possible on a gondola display

12.40

Which of the following statements **inaccurately** criticizes the practice of relating space allocations in a shop directly to sales?

A fast-moving lines and market leaders may not produce the best profit for the retailer

B the practice does not make the most efficient use of staff time

C displays dominated by fast-moving lines can give the impression of a narrow and/or mundane assortment

D it ignores the differential effects of display space in stimulating product sales

E none of these

12.41

Which of the following retail categories is likely to spend the greatest proportion of turnover on advertising?

A variety stores

B mail order houses

C chemists

D supermarkets

E newsagents

12.42

With vertical co-operation advertising:

A two or more retailers promote their advantages in common

B a supplier and a retailer promote the product(s) and the shop(s) jointly

C a specific product or range is advertised, and a number of retailers are listed with the advertisement

D the supplier is required to be the dominant partner

E the cost is always borne equally by the co-operators

12.43

Which of the following activities is **not** usually associated with the concept of retail sales promotion?

A new staff uniform

B contests

C celebrity appearance

D special display

E bonus points, according to size of purchase, redeemable for cash

12.44

A budget-priced children's clothes retailer is contemplating joining the Visa/MasterCard credit card system because several competitors now take these cards. He surveys fifty of his customers. Only five say they occasionally or regularly use credit cards. The retailer should:

A abandon the idea because of low customer interest

B reposition the shop to attract credit card customers

C try to estimate the effect on profits before deciding on adoption or rejection of the idea

D give a 2 per cent across-the-board discount to his customers (equivalent to about half the card service's commission on sales) to stay competitive

E carry out another survey in six months before finally deciding

12.45*

A company decides to give its sales assistants a flat 9 per cent commission on whatever they sell. The staff union complains that this has amounted to a 25 per cent cut in wage levels and has also 'undermined the company's premier asset, which is customer service'. Which of the following criticisms of the union's view would seem to be **unjustified**?

A a cut in wage levels is not necessarily synonymous with a cut in wages

B the union cannot prove that a cut in wage levels will undermine service

C the union is more concerned with wages than with service

D the union fails to take into account the company's overall marketing mix

E the union's statement takes no account of the company's competitive situation

12.46*

An integrated service policy is most important for which type of shop?

A full-service

B limited-service

C self-selection

D self-service

E equally important to all types

12.47

Which factors have been most influential in reducing the levels of retail staffing in recent years?

1 the desire to minimize wage costs

2 the view that advertising, packaging, and merchandising fulfil most of the functions of salespeople

3 the inability to find enough people suitable for sales work

4 the widespread introduction of point-of-sale computers

5 the view that customers are increasingly averse psychologically to the presence of sales staff

A 1 and 2

B 1 and 3

C 2 and 3

D 3 and 4

E 4 and 5

12.48

Which of the following statements is **not** accepted as a benefit of running an 'own label' store charge card (i.e. a card accepted only in that store or other stores of the chain)?

A offering the card attracts customers who previously did not patronize the store

B loyalty to the store tends to increase

C direct mail can be targeted to appeal to specific customer types

D other financial services can be developed and promoted

E detailed information can be gained about customer characteristics and spending patterns

12.49*

A **disadvantage** of the service life-cycle concept is that:

A it does not indicate what particular action to take if a service diminishes in need or importance

B it does not evaluate the differential advantage gained by introducing a new service

C it does not analyse the effects of copying of the service by competitors

D it does not examine the situation if all retailers in the sector offer the service

E it overlooks the effect of the institutionalization of the service over time

12.50*

Which of the following statements **incorrectly** compares physical products sold by a product retailer with service 'products' sold by a service retailer?

A physical products are produced and then sold, whereas service products are sold, then produced

B physical products may or may not be perishable, whereas service products are all perishable

C physical products are priced by entirely different methods than those used for service products

D physical products are standardized, whereas service products are non-standardized

E physical products are tangible, whereas service products are intangible

13

WHOLESALING

13.1
Which of the following statements **incorrectly** represents a difference between wholesalers and retailers?

A wholesalers pay less attention to promotion, atmosphere, and location than retailers

B wholesalers usually cover a larger trade area than retailers

C wholesalers deal with business customers, whereas retailers deal with final consumers

D wholesale prices are usually lower than retail prices

E wholesale transactions are usually smaller than retail transactions

13.2
Which of the following is **not** a benefit of wholesaling activities?

A dealing with wholesalers allows small or financially weak producers to avoid the great expense of operating a direct-selling organization

B wholesalers have a wider range of customer contacts and greater selling expertise than most producers

C wholesaling relieves the producer of the need to undertake marketing activities

D retailers carrying many lines often prefer to buy assortments from a wholesaler rather than from many producers

E wholesalers offer economies of scale

13.3
Wholesaler costs and profits are usually independent of which of the following?

A the legal form of the wholesaler's business

B the rate of inventory turnover

C the functions performed

D the wholesaler's efficiency

E the level of competition

13.4
Wholesalers do **not** usually qualify for which of the following discounts?

A trade discounts

B quantity discounts

C cash discounts

D allowances

E promotional discounts

13.5*
Which of the following is **not** a function generally performed by wholesalers?

A assortment gathering

B providing a trained sales force

C offering financing for manufacturers, retailers or institutional customers

D providing warehousing and delivery facilities

E bulk making

13.6
The wholesaler's role in physical distribution is likely to be important **except** where:

A a great many producers each produce numerous products in a given product class

B only a few producers dominate an industry

C manufacturer's brand is not an important consideration to the retailer

D numerous small independent retailers account for a large proportion of sales in the particular product class

E the lot size required by retailers tends to be small

13.7*
Which of the following have adversely affected wholesaling in recent years?

1 the spread of just-in-time (JIT) manufacturing practices

2 the increasing importance of retail multiples

3   an increase in the number of levels of intermediate producers and users

4   the growth of larger factories located some distance from the principal final buyers

5   the increasing need to adapt products to the needs of intermediate and final users in terms of quantities, packages, and forms

A 1 and 2

B 1 and 3

C 2 and 3

D 3 and 4

E 4 and 5

13.8*

The difference between a supplier selling **to** a wholesaler rather than **through** a wholesaler is that:

A selling to a wholesaler implies that the wholesaler is viewed as a customer who must be researched and satisfied, whereas selling through a wholesaler implies that retailers are the sole objects of the supplier's interest

B selling to a wholesaler implies that the wholesaler takes title to the goods, whereas selling through a wholesaler implies that the wholesaler does not take title

C selling to a wholesaler implies that the wholesaler determines who the final customers are to be, whereas selling through a wholesaler implies that the supplier determines this

D selling to a wholesaler implies that the wholesaler should be allowed to set the recommended final selling price, whereas selling through a wholesaler implies that the supplier should do this

E selling to a wholesaler implies that the supplier views the wholesaler as the final customer, whereas selling through a wholesaler implies that the supplier views the retailer as the final customer

13.9

From the marketing viewpoint, an **ineffective** customer-selection criterion for a wholesaler would be:

A any customer interested in the stock carried

B the customer's annual turnover

C the geographic location of the customer

D the customer's service requirements

E none of these

13.10

The 'product' sold by a wholesaler is best described as the wholesaler's:

A contacts with producers

B assortment of goods

C assortment of services

D assortment of goods and services

E convenience

13.11*

The most typical pricing method used by wholesalers is:

A target-return pricing

B perceived-value pricing

C going-rate pricing

D markup pricing

E psychological pricing

13.12*

A wholesaler previously operating under a low-cost, low-investment strategy takes the lead among wholesalers in its industry and decides to invest heavily in sophisticated technology, including automated warehouses, centralized inventory analysis, and direct computer links with suppliers and major customers. We may infer from this that the wholesaler's main intention is to:

A compete more effectively with other wholesalers in the industry

B become more cost-effective than manufacturers' sales branches

C reposition the company to deal only with up-market retailers

D improve its image and thereby attract new customers

E create a vertical marketing system

13.13

Which form of promotion is most relied upon by wholesalers?

A sales promotion

B trade advertising

C publicity

D personal selling

E direct mail

13.14*

Which of the following statements **incorrectly** compares manufacturer wholesaling with merchant wholesaling?

A the manufacturer controls wholesaling in manufacturer wholesaling, whereas the wholesaler controls wholesaling in merchant wholesaling

B the manufacturer performs all the wholesaling functions in manufacturer wholesaling, whereas the wholesaler may not perform all the wholesaling functions in merchant wholesaling

C the manufacturer receives payment when the goods are sold to the retailer or other customer in manufacturer wholesaling, whereas the wholesaler does not receive payment until the retailer or other customer sells the goods in merchant wholesaling

D the manufacturer owns the products that it sells to the retailer or other customer in manufacturer wholesaling, whereas the wholesaler owns the products that it sells to these customers in merchant wholesaling

E no inventory is held on the premises in some forms of merchant wholesaling, whereas inventory is held on the premises in merchant wholesaling

13.15

Which of the following conditions are **unlikely** to induce a manufacturer to undertake manufacturer wholesaling?

1 the manufacturer wants control over its marketing effort

2 customers are numerous and the average account size is small

3 the manufacturer is planning rapid expansion

4 customers are geographically clustered

5 a computerized order system links the manufacturer with its customers

A 1 and 2

B 1 and 3

C 2 and 3

D 3 and 4

E 4 and 5

13.16

Which is the odd one out?

A cash-and-carry wholesalers

B truck wholesalers

C drop shippers

D commission merchants

E none of these

13.17

Which of the following would we expect to carry the shallowest product lines?

A general-line wholesalers

B specialty-merchandise wholesalers

C rack jobbers

D general merchandise wholesalers

E cannot be determined

13.18

Which of the following would we expect to carry the widest product mix?

A general-line wholesalers

B specialty-merchandise wholesalers

C rack jobbers

D general merchandise wholesalers

E cannot be determined

13.19

Which of the following would we expect to carry the narrowest product mix?

A general-line wholesalers

B specialty-merchandise wholesalers

C rack jobbers

D general merchandise wholesalers

E cannot be determined

13.20*

Which of the following would we expect to carry the deepest product lines?

A general-line wholesalers

B specialty-merchandise wholesalers

C rack jobbers

D general merchandise wholesalers

E cannot be determined

13.21*

The trends towards concentrated ownership in retailing and the development of superstores specializing in mass merchandising are likely to pose the greatest threat to:

A general-line wholesalers

B specialty-merchandise wholesalers

C rack jobbers

D general merchandise wholesalers

E cannot be determined

13.22

Which of the following would **not** be carried by rack jobbers?

A paperback books

B hardware items

C health and beauty aids

D fresh fruit

E toys

Case Study 13.2
Super Valu

Super Valu is one of the biggest food wholesalers in the world, supplying around 4,500 supermarkets (many of them independent) in the United States. Super Valu calls itself the 'Retail Support Company', and provides its customers with credit, trains their employees, offers insurance coverage, instals computerized inventory systems, offers private-label items, and helps in shop design. The marketing roles of the partners are specified in legal agreements.

In recent years, the growth of Kroger, America's largest grocery retailer with almost 1,300 supermarkets and annual sales of around $22 billion, and its dynamic close rival, Wal-Mart, has put the squeeze on Super Valu, since both Kroger and Wal-Mart do their own warehousing. In 1993, Super Valu reacted by taking control of Wetterau, a grocery wholesaler that also runs supermarkets generating sales of $1.1 billion a year.

Questions 13.23–13.25 relate to this case study

13.23

Before the acquisition of Wetterau, Super Valu operated in the structure of:

A a traditional/conventional channel system

B an administered VMS

C a corporate VMS

D a contractual VMS

E a horizontal marketing system

13.24

In relation to Wetterau, Super Valu has created:

A a traditional/conventional channel system

B an administered VMS

C a corporate VMS

D a contractual VMS

E a horizontal marketing system

13.25

Super Valu's current marketing channel arrangements are in danger of encountering:

A channel incompatibility

B vertical channel conflict

C horizontal channel conflict

D multichannel conflict

E channel overload

13.26*

Which of the following services would we expect all limited-service merchant wholesalers to provide?

A trade credit

B merchandising assistance

C maintenance of a large inventory

D delivery of goods

E none of these

13.27*

Which of the following types of wholesalers experiences the lowest warehousing costs as a proportion of sales?

A truck wholesalers

B drop shippers

C rack jobbers

D mail-order wholesalers

E cash-and-carry wholesalers

13.28

Which of the following is the most suitable supplier for a car repair shop requiring small quantities of goods?

A truck wholesalers

B drop shippers

C rack jobbers

D mail-order wholesalers

E cash-and-carry wholesalers

13.29

Which of the following is likely to find that its main customers are located in small outlying areas and order in relatively small quantities?

A truck wholesalers

B drop shippers

C rack jobbers

D mail-order wholesalers

E cash-and-carry wholesalers

13.30*

Which of the following is likely to have the highest operating costs as a proportion of sales?

A truck wholesalers

B drop shippers

C rack jobbers

D mail-order wholesalers

E cash-and-carry wholesalers

13.31

Which of the following have no outside sales force?

1 truck wholesalers

2 drop shippers

3 rack jobbers

4 mail-order wholesalers

5 cash-and-carry wholesalers

A 1 and 2

B 1 and 3

C 2 and 3

D 3 and 4

E 4 and 5

13.32

Which of the following are characteristics of brokers and brokerage?

1 brokers work strictly on a commission basis

2 brokers have relatively high selling expenses

3 arrangements between brokers and the companies that use them are essentially short-term

4 brokers are paid for their services by the vendor of what is sold

5 products can be brokered, whereas services cannot

A 1 and 2

B 1 and 3

C 2 and 3

D 3 and 4

E 4 and 5

13.33

With which of the following intermediaries are prices **not** usually set by the vendor?

1 auction companies

2 manufacturers' agents

3 purchasing agents

4 selling agents

5 commission merchants

A 1 and 2

B 1 and 3

C 2 and 3

D 3 and 4

E 4 and 5

13.34

Which of the following intermediaries operate in a limited geographic territory?

A auction companies

B manufacturers' agents

C purchasing agents

D selling agents

E commission merchants

13.35*

Which of the following intermediaries perform the greatest range of marketing functions?

A auction companies

B manufacturers' agents

C purchasing agents

D selling agents

E commission merchants

13.36

Which of the following statements **incorrectly** characterizes manufacturers' agents?

A they represent two or more non-competing producers of complementary products

B they can help large producers to minimize the costs of developing new sales territories

C they are more cost-effective than a company sales force in areas with high market potential

D they are particularly useful to small producers having relatively few financial resources

E they can help large producers to adjust sales strategies for different products in different locations

Case Study 13.2
Wholesale power

A particular wholesaler is an important distributor of larger size women's clothing to independently-owned dress shops and boutiques on the East Coast and in the Mid-West of the United States. It has become aware that increasing costs of physical distribution, selling, service, and administration are absorbing a rising proportion of its gross margin, and although the market is growing, the situation is now starting to affect profits. At the same time, the wholesaler is reluctant to pass on all of the costs through higher prices because it fears that too great an increase will cause some customers to switch wholesalers, and others to reduce their order size. Therefore, the management has decided to ask two manufacturers in particular, whose goods together account for over 60 per cent of the wholesaler's annual sales, to reduce their prices. The wholesaler buys almost 90 per cent of the output of manufacturer A, and about 20 per cent (amounting to $5 million annually) of the output of manufacturer B. In both cases, the wholesaler has intimated that it may be forced to reduce future orders if the price reduction is not agreed.

Questions 13.37–13.41 relate to this case study

13.37*
In relation to manufacturer A, the wholesaler is attempting to exercise:

A reward power

B coercive power

C expert power

D referent power

E legitimate power

13.38*
In relation to manufacturer B, the wholesaler is attempting to exercise:

A reward power

B coercive power

C expert power

D referent power

E legitimate power

13.39
If manufacturer A offers to reduce prices so long as the wholesaler guarantees to increase its orders in the next twelve months by 5 per cent compared with the past twelve months, the manufacturer is attempting to exercise:

A reward power

B coercive power

C expert power

D referent power

E legitimate power

13.40
If manufacturer B replies that the wholesaler has been slow in paying accounts, and that the only help with price could be a special 3.5 per cent discount for payment strictly within thirty days of invoice, the manufacturer is attempting to exercise:

A reward power

B coercive power

C expert power

D referent power

E legitimate power

13.41*
Manufacturer B says that because of the wholesaler's persistent late payment, prices cannot be reduced now. However, the proposition will be reconsidered in six months if the wholesaler strictly observes the manufacturer's terms of trade during that period. The manufacturer is attempting to exercise:

A reward power

B coercive power

C expert power

D referent power

E legitimate power

13.42*
A men's clothing wholesaler provides a limited range of non-distribution services to independent retailers to help them in their operations. This is an example of the:

A traditional/conventional channel system

B administered VMS

C corporate VMS

D contractual VMS

E horizontal marketing system

13.43
Wholesaler-sponsored voluntary chains have been formed as a strategy to compete with:

A independent retailers

B small retail chains

C large retail chains

D small wholesalers

E large wholesalers

13.44

The main attractions to retailers of the wholesaler-sponsored voluntary chain are that:

1 the retailers have great influence on the strategic planning of the wholesaler

2 the retailers benefit from buying economies through group purchase

3 the merchandising programs developed by the wholesaler enhance the retailers' market presence

4 management fees payable by retailers are lower than with franchise arrangements

5 the retailers retain their individual identity

A 1 and 2

B 1 and 3

C 2 and 3

D 3 and 4

E 4 and 5

13.45*

An important difference between a manufacturer-wholesaler franchise and a wholesaler-retailer franchise is that:

A the former represents a contractual VMS, whereas the latter represents an administered VMS

B the former represents an administered VMS, whereas the latter represents a corporate VMS

C the former represents a traditional/conventional marketing channel, whereas the latter represents a contractual VMS

D the former represents an administered VMS, whereas the latter represents a contractual VMS

E none of these

13.46*

In a manufacturer-wholesaler franchise arrangement, we can expect the wholesaler to:

A specialize in niche marketing

B carry out only the distribution function

C be wholly- or partly-owned by the manufacturer

D carry out certain production processes as well as the distribution function

E wholly or partly own the manufacturer

13.47*

In a wholesaler-retailer franchise arrangement, we can expect the wholesaler to:

A be wholly- or partly-owned by the retailers

B wholly or partly own the retailers

C carry out only the distribution function

D carry out certain marketing functions as well as the distribution function

E represent only a single independent wholesaler as franchisor

13.48

A membership wholesale club (or warehouse club) differs from other forms of wholesaling in that:

A little service is offered

B it deals with ultimate consumers as well as the trade

C only a limited assortment of fast-selling items is carried

D merchandise usually is sold to the members before the club has to pay suppliers

E customers are not allowed any credit

13.49*

Which of the following statements **incorrectly** describes why it may be more advantageous for small suppliers to deal directly with a multiple retailer than with a wholesaler?

A small producers can greatly expand their market areas by dealing directly with multiple retailers

B small producers can greatly increase their volume of sales by dealing directly with multiple retailers

C multiple retailers can relieve small producers of the high costs of establishing extensive retail delivery systems

D small producers are likely to get a better price for their goods from multiple retailers than from wholesalers

E none of these statements is incorrect

13.50

Manufacturers' complaints that wholesalers do not carry enough inventory and therefore fail to fill customers' orders fast enough:

1 indicate that wholesalers are not meeting their commitments to manufacturers on volume targets

2 reflect manufacturers' hostility towards wholesaler niche marketing

3 go counter to the JIT philosophy adopted by many manufacturers

4 suggest that the problem may have to do more with wholesalers' forecasting, planning, and market intelligence than with stock-holding

5 are to some extent incongruous with manufacturers' complaints that wholesalers should reduce their costs

A 1 and 2

B 1 and 3

C 2 and 3

D 3 and 4

E 4 and 5

14
PROMOTION AND PROMOTIONAL STRATEGY

14.1
Which of the following promotional tools is best suited to a small audience?

A consumer promotion
B personal selling
C trade promotion
D advertising
E publicity

14.2
Which of the following is best suited to increase impulse purchases?

A consumer promotion
B personal selling
C trade promotion
D advertising
E publicity

14.3*
Which of the following is most likely to induce a retailer to provide shelf space for a new product?

A consumer promotion
B personal selling
C trade promotion
D advertising
E publicity

14.4
With which of the following does the sponsor have least control over content and placement?

A consumer promotion
B personal selling
C trade promotion
D advertising
E publicity

14.5
Which of the following generally costs the least per customer?

A consumer promotion
B personal selling
C trade promotion
D advertising
E publicity

14.6*
With which of the following promotional tools may the message vary from uniform to all customers, to specific to a given customer?

A consumer promotion
B personal selling
C trade promotion
D advertising
E publicity

14.7
With which of the following does the message depend entirely on who is the customer?

A consumer promotion
B personal selling
C trade promotion
D advertising
E publicity

14.8
Posters and leaflets are examples of which of the following?

A consumer promotion
B personal selling
C trade promotion
D advertising
E publicity

14.9

Which of the following would normally **not** play a role in communication strategy for consumer goods?

A the physical product itself

B the price of the product

C the product's brand

D the distribution system used in marketing the product

E the place from which the product is sold

14.10*

Marketing communication models expect marketing communications to meet all the following strategic requirements **except** to:

A try to estimate the effect of marketing messages on sales

B develop messages to communicate the benefits to the target audience

C formulate a product concept to meet consumer needs and identify the appropriate target audience

D determine the budget necessary to meet communication requirements

E transmit messages through print, broadcast media and salespeople

14.11

Which of the following is **not** considered by marketing communication models?

A the source of the message

B the message channel used

C when the message is transmitted

D the receiver of the message

E the effect of the message

14.12*

When Du Pont advertised its Stainmaster carpeting, it was decided not to mention the name of the chemical used to make the carpet resistant to stains since it would have little meaning to consumers seeing the advertisement. According to the communication model, this decision was taken in the process of:

A filtering noise

B decoding

C providing feedback

D encoding

E encouraging response

14.13*

The more the communicator and the audience share perceptions, the more effective the message is likely to be in terms of:

A filtering noise

B decoding

C providing feedback

D encoding

E encouraging response

14.14

Which of the following categories would be considered **not** to be part of the audience to receive a firm's television advertising message?

A the firm's investors

B the general public

C channel members

D the firm's employees

E all are part of the audience

14.15*

When a firm addresses its initial messages to opinion leaders in the hope that they will provide word-of-mouth communication to other consumers, this is an example of the:

A multi-step flow of communication

B two-step flow of communication

C one-step flow of communication

D two-sided message

E one-sided message

14.16*

When opinion leaders convey a message by word-of-mouth, and that message is rejected by the opinion receivers, this is an example of the:

A multi-step flow of communication

B two-step flow of communication

C one-step flow of communication

D two-sided message

E one-sided message

14.17

When Avis advertises that because they are 'only number 2' in car rentals, they try harder, what type of communication is being employed?

A multi-step flow of communication

B two-step flow of communication

C one-step flow of communication

D two-sided message

E one-sided message

14.18

Which of the following is **not** an example of noise in the communication process?

A the recipient of a direct-mail advertisement is not interested in the offer

B a salesperson misidentifies a product and gives incorrect information

C two consumers have a conversation during a television commercial

D a consumer waiting at a supermarket checkout counter sees a sale on a competitor's item

E all of these are examples of noise

14.19

Noise may interfere with the communication process:

A only at the encoding and decoding stages

B only at the decoding and feedback stages

C only at the encoding, transmission by the medium, and the decoding stages

D only at the transmission by the medium and feedback stages

E at any stage

14.20

A few days after seeing a toothpaste advertisement promising better defence against gum disease, a consumer looking for the brand in the local supermarket cannot remember which one it is. This is an example of:

A selective recall

B selective attention

C selective distortion

D selective exposure

E selective feedback

14.21*

Repetition of the key part of the message takes into account the phenomenon of:

A selective recall

B selective attention

C selective distortion

D selective exposure

E selective feedback

14.22

Emotional appeals are **least** effective when:

A the product being advertised is not particularly involving

B they are linked to product benefits

C a product has lost its uniqueness

D consumer anxieties about the product are high

E the product message is stronger than the emotional appeal

14.23

Which of the following is **untrue** about humorous advertising?

A humour is a good attention-getting device

B humour is likely to enhance the credibility of the advertiser

C humour may distract customers who use competitive products from developing arguments against the advertiser's brand

D humour is most effective when the message concentrates on the brand image rather than on product benefits

E humour tends to make the message more memorable

14.24*

Message ambiguity is most useful when:

1 consumers do not hold strong beliefs about the brand

2 the brand is not targeted to any particular segment

3 the advertiser wants consumers to project their own needs on to the brand

4 consumers do not perceive important differences between brands

5 the brand is not price-competitive

A 1 and 2

B 1 and 3

C 2 and 3

D 3 and 4

E 4 and 5

14.25*

Which of the following statements on communication effectiveness is **untrue**?

A communication can produce the most effective shifts on unfamiliar, lightly felt, peripheral issues which do not lie at the centre of the recipient's value system

B communication is more likely to be effective where the source is believed to have expertise, high status, objectivity, or likeability

C the greater the monopoly of the communication source over the message recipient, the greater the change or effect in favour of the source over the recipient

D communication effects are greatest where the message is in line with the existing opinions, beliefs, and dispositions of the receiver

E the social context, group, or reference group most often has very little influence on whether the communication is accepted

14.26

The first step in promotional planning and strategy is to:

A work out product strategy

B identify the target audience

C establish promotional objectives

D determine the promotional budget

E evaluate the competition

14.27

In the various models of the adoption process in consumer decision-making, which of the following terms relate to the cognitive stage?

1 trial

2 awareness

3 exposure

4 interest

5 conviction

A 1 and 2

B 1 and 3

C 2 and 3

D 3 and 4

E 4 and 5

14.28

In the various models of the adoption process in consumer decision-making, which of the following terms relate to the affective stage?

1 trial

2 awareness

3 exposure

4 interest

5 conviction

A 1 and 2

B 1 and 3

C 2 and 3

D 3 and 4

E 4 and 5

14.29*

A communicator's attempt to take prospective buyers through the sequence of 'learning', to 'doing', to 'feeling' is most appropriate:

A when the audience has low involvement with a product category but perceives high differentiation within the product category

B when the audience has high involvement with a product category and perceives high differentiation within the product category

C when the audience has high involvement with a product category but perceives little or no differentiation within the product category

D when the audience has low involvement with a product category and perceives little or no differentiation within the product category

E cannot be determined

14.30

A communicator's attempt to take prospective buyers through the sequence of 'learning', to 'feeling', to 'doing' is most appropriate:

A when the audience has low involvement with a product category but perceives high differentiation within the product category

B when the audience has high involvement with a product category and perceives high differentiation within the product category

C when the audience has high involvement with a product category but perceives little or no differentiation within the product category

D when the audience has low involvement with a product category and perceives little or no differentiation within the product category

E cannot be determined

14.31*

In the product categories of aluminum house siding or window double-glazing, the communicator would be well advised to try to move prospective buyers through the sequence of:

A 'learning' to 'feeling' to 'doing'

B 'feeling' to 'doing' to 'learning'

C 'doing' to 'feeling' to 'learning'

D 'doing' to 'learning' to 'feeling'

E 'learning' to 'doing' to 'feeling'

14.32

In the innovation-adoption model, personal sources of information, particularly relatives and friends, are likely to be most important to prospective purchasers during which stages of the adoption process?

1 evaluation

2 awareness

3 trial

4 interest

5 adoption

A 1 and 2

B 1 and 3

C 2 and 3

D 3 and 4

E 4 and 5

14.33*

For which of the following groups would a message geared towards overcoming caution and deliberation be most appropriate?

A late majority

B early majority

C laggards

D innovators

E early adopters

14.34

Personal selling is likely to be the **least** cost-effective promotional tool at which stage of the PLC?

A introduction

B growth

C maturity

D decline

E cannot be determined

14.35

Consumer promotion is likely to be at its most cost-effective at which stage of the PLC?

A introduction

B growth

C maturity

D decline

E cannot be determined

14.36*

Which of the following **cannot** usually be considered a valid long-term objective of communication strategy?

A to build brand awareness

B to increase the frequency of use of a brand

C to increase a brand's market share

D to encourage non-users to try a brand

E to educate consumers in how to use a product

Case Study 14.1
Power in promotional strategy

Some months in advance of the British launch of Persil Power concentrated washing powder by Lever, Procter & Gamble began to badge some of its washing products with slogans emphasizing the word 'power'. For example, Ariel Liquid was said to have 'Extra **power** to remove stains'. When Persil Power in biological and non-biological formats was introduced in summer 1994, newspaper advertisements for Ariel and Fairy (both Procter & Gamble brands) attacked Persil's innovation, a manganese accelerator said to improve cleaning performance. No direct mention of Persil was made in the advertisements.

The advertisement for Ariel Ultra biological powder stressed that it contained no accelerator. The advertisement claimed that independent fabric safety tests proved that Ariel was much kinder to some clothes than powders with high levels of the manganese accelerator. According to the advertisement, the latest version of these powders had lower levels of the manganese accelerator, but they didn't reduce the unwanted effects of holes and tears on vulnerable viscose and heavily coloured cotton. A photograph was used to substantiate the claimed deleterious effects of using the powder with accelerator instead of Ariel Ultra. Readers were warned that accelerator residues can be left on clothes, and 'even if you stop using these products and change back to Ariel, you could still see colour damage to vulnerable clothes resulting from the effects of the manganese accelerator'. The advertisement concludes, 'Now you know why only Ariel washes so clean yet so safe.'

The same claims were repeated in relation to non-biological powders in the Fairy powder advertisement: powders with high levels of manganese accelerators were no longer made, but the risk of damage was still there with non-biological powders containing lower levels of the accelerator; Fairy Non-Bio contained no accelerator; even if you change back to Fairy from accelerator non-bios, you could still see colour damage.

Why this aerial bombardment?

Sorry about the warfare. It wasn't our idea.

Our idea was simply for a better washing powder. We call it Persil Power. Families all over Britain have already used it in more than fifty million washes. And they love the results.

Meanwhile, we asked independent test institutes to compare Persil Power with another leading concentrated powder. They found no visible sign of fabric damage with either product.

VISCOSE BLOUSE WASHED 50 TIMES AT 40°C IN PERSIL POWER.

Some of them did find a difference, even so. And that difference was Persil Power's significantly superior cleaning performance.

So use Persil Power with confidence. We always knew it would start a washing revolution.

We just didn't expect it to start a war.

Persil POWER

New Persil Power gets out more tough stains first time at low temperatures.

 A LEVER GUARANTEED PRODUCT   WE TRUST YOU'LL BE HAPPY WITH EVERY PERSIL PRODUCT SO, AS ALWAYS, WE OFFER A FULL MONEY BACK GUARANTEE. STATUTORY RIGHTS NOT AFFECTED.

Fig. 14.1 Persil's reply to comparative advertising in the powder power war
(used by permission)

Lever, which prefers to use television rather than press advertising to sell washing powder, nevertheless quickly responded in the same newspapers that carried the Ariel and Fairy advertisements (Figure 14.1). Persil Power's advertisement observed the current British rules restricting the use of registered trade marks in comparative advertising, but with tongue in cheek, mentioned the 'aerial bombardment'. It apologised about the warfare which, it said, was not its idea. The advertisement reported that Persil Power had been used in over fifty million washes, and families all over Britain loved the results. According to Persil, independent test institutes compared Persil Power with another leading concentrated powder, and found no visible sign of fabric damage with either product. The only difference that some detected was Persil Power's significantly superior cleaning performance. A photograph of an unfaded, perfectly intact viscose blouse washed fifty times in Persil was used to demonstrate the point. The advertisement concluded, 'So use Persil Power with confidence. We always knew it would start a washing revolution. We just didn't expect it to start a war.'

Questions 14.37–14.39 relate to this case study

14.37

The Ariel and Fairy advertisements appear to have which of the following objectives?

1 to try to get rejectors of Ariel and Fairy to retry the brand
2 to change the basis for comparing Ariel and Fairy on one hand with Persil Power on the other
3 to reinforce customer loyalty to Ariel and Fairy
4 to reposition Ariel and Fairy
5 to change the brand preference of those who use Persil Power

A 1 and 2
B 1 and 3
C 2 and 3
D 3 and 4
E 4 and 5

14.38

The Persil Power advertisement appears to have which of the following objectives?

1 to encourage brand loyalty among Ariel Power users
2 to knock the Ariel and Fairy brands
3 to correct misconceptions about the brand

4 to calm apprehensions of investors and channel members
5 to encourage non-users to try Persil Power

A 1 and 2
B 1 and 3
C 2 and 3
D 3 and 4
E 4 and 5

14.39*

Which of the following statements **incorrectly** characterizes comparative advertising?

A most comparative advertising is one-sided
B comparative advertising can lead to more rational purchase decisions
C comparative advertising is more likely to be successful when a challenger attacks a leader
D comparative advertising is more persuasive than non-comparative advertising
E there is a tendency with comparative advertising for consumers to misidentify the sponsor of the advertisement

14.40*

Which of the following is **not** a shortcoming of the use of marginal analysis in the short-run determination of promotional outlay?

A marginal analysis measures response only in terms of sales, whereas promotion may have non-sales objectives
B it is extremely difficult to determine where the marginal profit from the last promotional pound will just equal the marginal profit from the last pound in the best non-promotional use
C marginal analysis assumes full knowledge of the shape of the response function, but in reality only educated guesses can be made
D short-run marginal analysis overlooks the fact that promotional outlay continues to work for a period in the future
E by focusing on profit, marginal analysis fails to measure more important aspects of business activity

14.41

A marketer believes that by spending the same percentage of his firm's sales on advertising as his competitors, he will be able to maintain market share. He is using which method to determine promotional allocation?

A arbitrary allocation method

B objective-and-task method

C competitive parity method

D all-you-can-afford method

E percentage of sales method

14.42

The promotional budgeting method that requires management to spell out its assumptions about the relationship between promotional expenditure, exposure levels, trial rates, and regular usage is the:

A arbitrary allocation method

B objective-and-task method

C competitive parity method

D all-you-can-afford method

E percentage of sales method

14.43

When a marketer has to bargain with the company's finance department over how much can be allocated to promotion, which budgeting method is being employed?

A arbitrary allocation method

B objective-and-task method

C competitive parity method

D all-you-can-afford method

E percentage of sales method

14.44*

Which of the following statements **incorrectly** criticizes the distinction made between above-the-line and below-the-line promotion?

A there is no radical difference between the purpose and effect of expenditure above and below the line in terms of the brand

B the distinction is not useful in differentiating between push and pull promotional techniques

C it is a false dichotomy, since many below-the-line promotions are dependent on above-the-line support

D the distinction is meaningless in terms of the way a consumer sees a brand

E using the distinction tends to inhibit the creation of an integrated approach to promotional planning

14.45*

Which of the following considerations is normally **unimportant** in determining the weight promotion should receive in the total marketing mix?

A whether the products are commodities or highly differentiable products

B where the company's products are in their life cycles

C whether the products are routinely needed

D whether the products are simple or complex

E how much the products sell for on average

14.46*

Which of the following statements **incorrectly** characterize the promotional mix?

1 there is only one best way to mix promotional elements for a given target market

2 a single promotional mix is normally sufficient for one product, even if the company is targeting more than one market

3 one promotional tool can be substituted for another in a promotional mix

4 the elements of a promotional mix can be changed in the short run, as the need arises

5 one promotional tool can be used to promote another in a promotional mix

A 1 and 2

B 1 and 3

C 2 and 3

D 3 and 4

E 4 and 5

14.47

In determining the promotional mix, which element is usually established first?

A personal selling

B publicity

C advertising

D consumer promotion

E trade promotion

14.48

A company with a short-term focus is likely to concentrate its promotion on:

A personal selling

B publicity

C advertising

D consumer promotion

E trade promotion

14.49*

Customer conviction is influenced:

A mostly by personal selling, and less by advertising and consumer promotion

B almost entirely by personal selling and consumer promotion

C mostly by advertising and publicity, and less by personal selling and consumer promotion

D primarily by advertising and personal selling

E mainly by personal selling and consumer promotion, but also somewhat by reminder advertising

14.50

Which of the following are used in a 'push' strategy?

1 consumer promotion

2 publicity

3 trade promotion

4 personal selling

5 advertising

A 1 and 2

B 1 and 3

C 2 and 3

D 3 and 4

E 4 and 5

15

ADVERTISING, PUBLIC RELATIONS, AND PUBLICITY

15.1
Which of the following statements **incorrectly** characterizes advertising?

A advertising attracts a geographically dispersed audience

B advertisers have a broad range of media from which to choose

C advertising delivers a uniform message to the entire audience

D advertising can increase an audience's liking for a firm's brands

E advertising costs per person reached tend to be high

15.2*
Advertising is normally particularly effective:

A for homogeneous products lacking unique features

B when the number of prospective users is relatively small

C if not all product benefits are apparent to consumers on inspection and use of the product

D when a company with a small market share is challenging the market leader

E under all these conditions

15.3
An emphasis on advertising as the main promotional tool is most likely in all the following cases **except** when products:

A are high in price

B are standardized and aimed at mass markets

C have easily communicated features

D are new

E are sold through independent channel members

15.4*
Word-of-mouth advertising has been rejected as 'true' advertising by advertising theorists because:

1 it can convey negative information

2 it is personal, as opposed to non-personal, communication

3 the communication lacks defined sponsorship

4 the communication tends to be product-centred

5 word-of-mouth communication lacks persuasiveness

A 1 and 2

B 1 and 3

C 2 and 3

D 3 and 4

E 4 and 5

15.5*
An advertisement for British Rail Inter City services shows a train speeding past long lines of stationary cars caught in rush-hour traffic on the motorway. This is an example of:

A reinforcement advertising

B competitive advertising

C defensive advertising

D institutional advertising

E comparative advertising

15.6
Advertising by Seagram distillers to promote the idea that drinking and driving do not mix is an example of:

A reinforcement advertising

B competitive advertising

C defensive advertising

D institutional advertising

E comparative advertising

15.7
Which of the following would **not** be found in pioneer advertising?

A   a comparison between brands

B   an illustration of how the product can be used

C   an indication of where the product can be purchased

D   information on product benefits

E   all of these can be found

15.8*

Which of the following advertising objectives is the odd one out?

A   announcing a price change

B   changing the customer's perception of product attributes

C   building a company image

D   correcting false impressions

E   describing available services

15.9

The American Express slogan, 'Don't leave home without it', is an example of:

A   reminder advertising

B   persuasive advertising

C   product advertising

D   informative advertising

E   co-operative advertising

15.10*

Which of the following objectives of advertising may exhibit a trade-off relationship?

1   to increase product sales

2   to increase expenditure by existing customers

3   to increase store traffic

4   to upgrade the store image

5   to attract new customers

A   1 and 2

B   1 and 3

C   2 and 3

D   3 and 4

E   4 and 5

15.11

Which of the following factors would **not** normally influence the development of specific advertising objectives?

A   competitive advertising campaigns

B   the advertisement's degree of creativity

C   the original selection of a target market segment

D   opportunities in the marketplace

E   the product's stage in the PLC

15.12*

The task of a promotional window is to:

A   sell the store

B   sell merchandise

C   sell items and ideas not related to the store

D   advertise price reductions

E   none of these

15.13

Retail advertising dominated by numerous price reduction announcements, with little attention given to the promotion of other store attributes, tend to:

1   enhance customer loyalty

2   result in poor attribution of advertising claims

3   encourage limited or complex decision-making

4   strengthen message credibility

5   be more effective as a long-term strategy than a short-term tactic

A   1 and 2

B   1 and 3

C   2 and 3

D   3 and 4

E   4 and 5

15.14

Which advertising medium has the strategic function of reinforcing brand image and the tactical function of merchandising the product?

A   transit

B   point of purchase

C   television

D   daily newspaper

E   outdoor

15.15*

Message prominence is lowest with which advertising medium?

A   transit

B   point of purchase

C   television

D   daily newspaper

E   outdoor

15.16
Which advertising medium usually advertises the message without clutter from competing messages?

A transit

B point of purchase

C television

D daily newspaper

E outdoor

15.17*
Which of the following statements is **untrue** of national magazine advertising?

A it is more appropriate for large, rather than small, retailers

B it is not usually suitable for those seeking geographic segmentation

C it has a longer lead-time than does national newspaper advertising

D the principles of advertisement positioning are the same as for newspapers

E none of these

15.18*
According to advertising theory, which is the most desirable position for a one-eighth page advertisement on an inside page of a newspaper?

A island position

B buried position

C anywhere above the fold

D next-to-reading position

E the full position

15.19
Kellogg decides on a national promotion of its various types of Rice Krispies, and offers its retailer customers special displays for the promotional packages. Retailers who use the displays in most cases want to:

A keep up with the competition

B expand their target market

C obtain a differential advantage in the marketplace

D alter their shop image

E reduce dependence on own brands

15.20*
Which of the following statements **incorrectly** characterizes the relationship between attitudes and a consumer's response to advertising?

A when consumers have a positive attitude toward an advertisement, they are more likely to have a positive attitude toward the advertised brand

B peripheral cues, such as an advertisement's imagery or background, are useful for creating positive feelings for low involvement products

C a disliked advertisement is capable of producing a positive consumer response

D when considering an advertised claim, a consumer is more likely to think of support arguments or counter arguments in low involvement situations

E product trial is a much stronger predictor of brand attitudes than is advertising exposure

15.21
Which of the following advertising themes would be most appropriate for products targeted to professionals and managers (the upper-middle and upper class)?

1 impressions of energy

2 security

3 solutions to practical problems in daily requirements

4 exclusiveness

5 self-expressive aims

A 1 and 2

B 1 and 3

C 2 and 3

D 3 and 4

E 4 and 5

15.22
Advertisements treating the product not as an objective entity but rather as a subjective symbol may be appropriate for marketing:

A cars

B cosmetics

C clothing

D sports equipment

E all of these

15.23*
Which of the following statements **incorrectly** characterizes the effects of repetition of an advertising message?

A repetition can enhance attitude change, but not behaviour change

B if a brand is not in a dominant position, repetition creates more awareness relative to market leaders

C   repetition can create such an ingrained image of a brand that any subsequent attempt to change it will be difficult

D   as advertising is repeated, the incremental gains in consumer retention become smaller

E   if competitive advertising is intense, repetition is required to maintain brand visibility

15.24

Advertising messages normally have the greatest difficulty in persuading consumers who:

A   are low in self-esteem and require social approval for their behaviour

B   are low in anxiety

C   exhibit social withdrawal tendencies

D   exhibit aggressive feelings

E   have fertile imaginations

15.25

Which of the following statements **fails** to explain why it is difficult to relate sales and profits to advertising?

A   advertising has a long-term effect on sales, and it is difficult to distinguish the effects of past advertising from that of the current campaign

B   advertising is not always intended to result in sales or profits

C   advertising is usually only one of many influences on the consumer

D   advertising is never intended to produce an immediate sales response

E   advertising is usually only one of the variables in the marketing mix

15.26

Which of the following criteria is **inappropriate** for communication-related advertising evaluation?

A   the extent to which the target market has been reached

B   the extent to which the product has increased its market share

C   the extent to which awareness of the product's benefits has increased in the target market

D   the extent to which consumers can remember any advertisements they saw the day before

E   the extent to which the advertisement generated inquiries about the product

Case Study 15.1
The Wonderbra

Gossard, a leading British and European lingerie brand, produced the Wonderbra, a push-up bra, under a twenty-five year world-wide licence from 1969 to 1993. The bra was originally designed to enhance the shape and cleavage of smaller-busted women, but the style was so popular that larger sizes were eventually introduced. The bra was marketed as 'the Gossard Wonderbra'. Under Gossard, the advertising slogans tended to be catchy and witty, for example at the start of the 1990s, 'say goodbye to your feet'.

In 1994, marketing of the Wonderbra passed to a leading international brand, Playtex, through Sara Lee (Playtex's parent company), which now controlled the licence through corporate acquisition. When Playtex launched its Wonderbra in the UK in January 1994, the bra, unlike other Playtex products, had a separate identity from other Playtex brands and made no reference to Playtex on its packaging. The advertising merely stated that this was 'the one and only Wonderbra, the original push-up plunge bra'. It was very similar to the Gossard version, but was said by Playtex to have much improved aesthetics designed to heighten consumer appeal. An extensive outdoor poster campaign was used to back the launch (see the example in Figure 15.1). Meanwhile, in January 1994, Gossard used television to launch its replacement product, 'the ultimate cleavage' Gossard Ultrabra, said to 'knock the stuffing out of ordinary bras' (see Figure 15.2).

The advertisements for the Wonderbra and Gossard Ultrabra were criticized by some as supposedly treating women as sex objects. However, the poster and advertising authorities did not uphold the complaints, agreeing with the view that the models were bold, confident women, and the context was humorous rather than offensive. Marcelle D'Argy Smith, editor of *Cosmopolitan*, concurred, adding, 'Breasts are big. I think the ads are wonderful.'

Questions 15.27–15.28 relate to this case study

15.27

Playtex's decision not to identify the Wonderbra with the corporate name appears to be based on which consideration?

A   to protect the corporate brand image in the event that the Wonderbra brand failed

B   to maintain certain specific existing Wonderbra brand values without causing customer confusion

C   to appeal to a different segment of the market from the Gossard Wonderbra

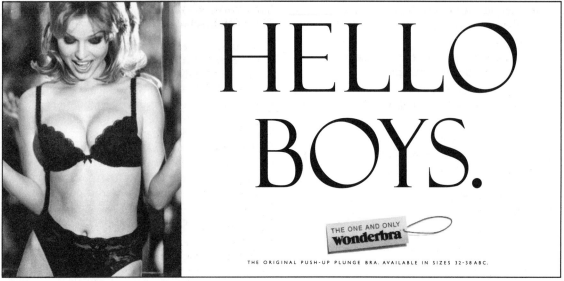

Fig. 15.1

KNOCKS THE STUFFING OUT OF ORDINARY BRAS

Playtex and Gossard display their wares
(used by permission)

Fig. 15.2

D to benefit from the economies of scale in advertising

E to differentiate its product from the Gossard Wonderbra

15.28

Which of the following statements **incorrectly** explains the effects of humour in advertising personal or ego-linked products?

A fears or anxieties connected with a product may be lessened by humour, thereby making the consumer more responsive to the message

B when humour dominates an advertising message, message comprehension and communication of product benefits both normally increase

C if humour does not treat the advertised product with respect, the message is unlikely to be effective

D humour is most effective in an advertising message when it has a natural association with the product

E none of these

Case Study 15.2
Advertising expenditure

In 1993, the average total promotional expenditure for a top-10 grocery brand in Britain was £15 million, about 7 per cent of sales. For the top 70 as a whole, it was £8 million, or more than 10 per cent of sales. Between 30 and 40 per cent of promotional outlay went on advertising. Of advertising expenditure, the press accounted for more than 60 per cent, and television, for more than 30 per cent. For the decade from 1982, the trend was for retail prices to rise by only about 60 per cent of the rate of increase of media costs. That, and other effects of the UK recession, help explain why British advertising spending fell by almost 17 per cent between 1989 and 1991.

Questions 15.29–15.30 relate to this case study

15.29*

From the information in the case study, we can deduce that:

1 advertising expenditure may act as a barrier to entry for new brands

2 companies that advertise throughout a recession win market share and become more profitable than those that do not

3 among the top 70 brands, the positive relationship between size of brand on one hand, and the ratio of sales to advertising and promotion on the other, may be in part due to a two-way causation process

4 competitive brand advertising is not to increase market share but to prevent the erosion of sales levels

5 in recent years, fewer products have been getting sufficient support during launch to create a defensible franchise

A 1 and 2

B 1 and 3

C 2 and 3

D 3 and 4

E 4 and 5

15.30

If a manufacturer producing numerous brands reacts to the cost pressures of advertising by deciding to maintain the total promotional budget but concentrate on sales promotion at the expense of advertising:

A this will probably result in an improved consumer disposition to the brands

B consumers' perceptions of the brands' added values may diminish

C the strategy should be confined to brands at the introduction or growth phase of the PLC

D the manufacturer's corporate identity may weaken in consumers' minds

E the effectiveness of the overall promotional effort will increase

Case Study 15.3
Irish stout

In mid-1994, Guinness Irish stout held about 80 per cent of the British stout market. Its television advertisement, repeated on and off during the summer, was relatively short and abandoned the story-line format typical of its advertisements for the past few years. Making scant and unspoken reference to the brand name, the advertisement dwelled on the written and unspoken established slogan, 'Pure Genius'. The television advertising for Murphy's Irish stout, a relatively recent introduction to Britain, depicted an otherwise disappointed young Irish man holding a pint of the drink but confiding to the audience, 'like the Murphy's, I'm not bitter'. In September 1994, Beamish Irish stout began a £4 million advertising campaign, starting with 1,800 large outdoor poster sites, to launch its stout, which is brewed in Cork, Ireland. In one advertisement, the main emphasis was on the word 'Corker', with less prominence given to the phrase '(not a Londoner)' appearing below it to the left of a large representation of a pint of stout with the Beamish logo on the glass. At the foot of the poster was the caption, 'the only draught stout brewed only in Ireland only'.

Questions 15.31–15.33 relate to this case study

15.31
The advertising strategy used by Guinness appears to centre on:

A increasing the consumer's product involvement

B changing the brand image

C communicating information

D reinforcing the brand image

E improving brand attitude

15.32
By implying that its stout was not as bitter as Guinness, the advertising strategy used by Murphy's appears to centre on:

A changing the consumer's image of Murphy's

B introducing a product on the basis of imagery

C reducing risk and uncertainty

D emphasizing a new feature for an existing product

E reminding consumers of the brand

15.33*
Which of the following propositions **cannot** be inferred from the approach used by Beamish in its launch?

A the company will make additional efforts to increase brand awareness

B the company believes that consumers seek functional values when selecting a stout

C most consumers are unaware that Guinness and Murphy's are brewed outside Ireland

D Beamish's launch is attempting to create brand awareness and message comprehension simultaneously

E the company believes that the origin of a stout is an important consumer selection criterion

15.34*
Which of the following activities is **not** a function of public relations?

A advising company management about public issues, company positions and image

B trying to influence legislators and government officials to promote or defeat legislation and regulation

C organizing training programmes for company employees to stimulate more effective contact with the public

D suggesting opportunities for new product development on the basis of marketing research

E all of these are public relations functions

15.35
Which of the following is **inappropriate** as an objective of public relations in marketing?

A assisting in repositioning a mature product

B influencing specific target customer groups

C providing a trigger for purchasing a product

D building up interest in a product category

E enhancing the corporate image

15.36*
A company has decided to introduce a carbonated soft drink containing a relatively high proportion of pure fruit juice. Which of the following objectives would be appropriate for this company's public relations campaign?

1 to have 50 per cent of all retailers making use of a special end-of-aisle display

2 to have 80 per cent of the shareholders aware and supportive of the company's new product introduction

3 to convince 60 per cent of school nutritionists that the brand should be available in soft drink machines on school premises because of health benefits

4 to stimulate trial by 40 per cent of the target market

5 to increase brand awareness to 80 per cent

A 1 and 2

B 1 and 3

C 2 and 3

D 3 and 4

E 4 and 5

15.37
Which of the following tasks is beyond the competence of public relations in marketing?

A to hold down promotion costs

B to increase the credibility of the sponsor's message

C to co-ordinate the timing of media exposure with a product launch

D to stimulate the salesforce and dealers

E to improve awareness of a product or service

15.38*

The target of a company's public relations effort should:

A be synonymous with the total buyer market targeted by the company

B depend on the objectives of the communication task

C be entirely external to the company

D normally be those who are hard to reach by means of other promotional tools

E focus on ultimate consumers and the community at large

15.39

Which of the following is **not** a public relations tool?

A the corporate symbol

B free parking

C a press conference

D a free guided tour of a factory

E the company trading name

15.40

A pressure group attacks a company over alleged malpractices. The company responds by promptly answering every critical comment in a properly counter- balanced general statement. In addition, the managing director writes individual replies to each of the newspapers and television and radio stations that carried the original critical story. The company's response is an example of:

A routine corporate public relations

B cause-related public relations

C proactive public relations

D reactive public relations

E third-party endorsement public relations

15.41

In mid-1994, large circular cardboard signs, resembling warning road signs, began to appear, tied to lamp posts every half mile or so, along major roads in British cities. Within each sign's red circular border was a message in large bold type: 'Warning. Climate Change Ahead'. Beneath this message was the sponsor's name in smaller green capital letters, GREENPEACE. This campaign is an example of:

A routine corporate public relations

B cause-related public relations

C proactive public relations

D reactive public relations

E third-party endorsement public relations

15.42

A monthly church newsletter is an example of:

A routine corporate public relations

B cause-related public relations

C proactive public relations

D reactive public relations

E third-party endorsement public relations

15.43

Which of the following is **not** an example of sponsorship?

A a manufacturer paying two pence to the British Olympic Committee for every returned proof of purchase from a special product package

B a tobacco company financing a Formula One racing team

C a large retailer endowing a university Chair of Retailing named after the company

D a company making a large donation to the Royal Opera House, Covent Garden

E a small retailer buying the uniforms and paying the travelling expenses for a local under 12's football team

15.44

Which of the following **incorrectly** explains the increasing importance in recent years of public relations as a marketing tool?

A media costs have been rising

B the power of mass advertising has been weakening because of increasing clutter

C editorial copy has been found to have considerably more influence than advertising

D the effectiveness of public relations is now easier to evaluate than advertising

E the slowdown in consumer spending has led many companies to limit or cut their advertising budgets

15.45*

Public relations differs from publicity in that:

A public relations may be paid or non-paid, whereas publicity is only non-paid

B public relations can be used for marketing support activities, whereas publicity cannot

C   public relations is demand- or image-oriented, whereas publicity is only image-oriented

D   public relations involves only non-personal communication, whereas publicity involves either personal or non-personal communication

E   all of these are differences

15.46

Publicity differs from advertising in that:

1   the sponsor has no choice of media for publicity, but has for advertising

2   publicity deals with 'newsworthy' matters, whereas advertising does not

3   publicity has less authority than advertising

4   publicity cannot be controlled by the sponsor, whereas advertising can

5   publicity is not paid for by the sponsor, whereas advertising is

A   1 and 2

B   1 and 3

C   2 and 3

D   3 and 4

E   4 and 5

15.47*

Which of the following are **not** aspects of publicity?

1   a customer relations department

2   an appeal for disaster relief

3   a company announcement of a revolutionary new product

4   fairs and trade shows

5   personal appearances

A   1 and 2

B   1 and 3

C   2 and 3

D   3 and 4

E   4 and 5

Case Study 15.4
Barbara Pepper Lingerie

A fourteenth-century inn in Nottingham, England, was redeveloped towards the end of the 1980s into a seventeen-unit shopping arcade costing £8 million. One of the first tenants, Barbara Pepper Lingerie, had been in a number of disputes with the landlord. The first involved the landlord's refusal to let the owners name the shop Bumps & Boobs, like their other four shops, on the grounds that it clashed with the arcade's upmarket image. The second dispute flared up over a poster of a rather large woman in underwear in the shop's window display, which the landlord demanded should be removed. The third dispute developed in the run-up to the official opening of the arcade in March 1989 (the arcade was still half-let and had been functioning for over a year), and involved, among other things, the enhanced incentives being given to entice new tenants.

In the face of poor trading results and an impasse with the landlord, the shop's owners decided to use a 'man bites dog' tactic to gain maximum attention at the official opening. On the day that British television star Jan Harvey opened the arcade, Barbara Pepper Lingerie put large fluorescent-coloured signs in the shop's windows announcing its 'Closing Down Sale'. The shop's owners provided a full press statement and were also interviewed by the press. The next day, the tabloid *Nottingham Evening Post* devoted 40 per cent of its front page to the arcade's opening, and focused in the text on Barbara Pepper's closing down. The story ignored the motives for the closure, but mentioned the previous rows and highlighted the shop's low and slashed prices several times. A spokesman for the landlords was interviewed and stated that the gesture had not marred the lavish and spectacular opening, which had attracted hundreds of people. Moreover, he regarded the closure as 'a positive move' since, he claimed, the shop did not 'sit comfortably' with the other tenants. In the next few months, before the shop finally closed, its trading results and its relations with the landlord improved somewhat.

Questions 15.48–15.49 relate to this case study

15.48*

Which of the following statements regarding reportage appear to be borne out by the case study?

1   public relations is more suitable to create a positive image than to correct a negative image

2   novelty themes are likely to attract more media interest than more usual 'media events'

3   publicity and public relations often exist symbiotically to gain media attention

4   reportage arising from publicity is easier for the sponsor to control than reportage arising for public relations events

5   special events are less effective as promotional tools than is publicity

A 1 and 2

B 1 and 3

C 2 and 3

D 3 and 4

E 4 and 5

15.49

From the case study, it appears that the target of the shop's publicity effort was:

A ultimate consumers

B the general public

C the landlord

D ultimate consumers and the landlord

E the general public and the landlord

15.50

Which of the following methods is **unsuitable** for evaluating the success of a publicity campaign:

A evaluating the effect of the campaign on company image

B analyzing the length and placement of coverage of each story

C comparing the desired with the actual timing of the story's appearance

D determining the cost of the campaign

E counting the media covering each story

16

SALES PROMOTION, PERSONAL SELLING, AND SALES MANAGEMENT

16.1
In comparing advertising with sales promotion:

A advertising offers a reason to buy, whereas sales promotion gives an incentive to buy

B advertising offers buyers an explanation of what is for sale, whereas sales promotion gives them a reason for buying

C advertising gives an incentive to buy, whereas sales promotion directs buyers to a particular brand

D advertising offers a sales premise, whereas sales promotion offers a sales purpose

E advertising and sales promotion both create buyer readiness

16.2
In which cases would a firm be best advised to use sales promotion rather than advertising for a product?

1 if there is high differentiation in the product category

2 if the product holds a dominant market share

3 if the product is in the maturity phase of the PLC

4 if the competition is promotion-oriented

5 if there is high purchase frequency of the product

A 1 and 2

B 1 and 3

C 2 and 3

D 3 and 4

E 4 and 5

16.3*
In recent years, which of the following factors has **not** inclined major consumer-packaged-goods companies increasingly to favour sales promotion over advertising as the main component in their promotional mixes?

A the desire by some companies to prefer fixed rather than variable promotional costs

B product managers are under greater pressure to increase current sales

C consumers are increasingly deal oriented

D pressure from large retailers exerting their buying power

E the number of brands has increased

16.4*
In planning promotional spending in the 1990s, marketing managers of large consumer-goods companies tend first to estimate what they need to spend in:

A trade promotion, then what they need to spend in consumer promotion, and then allocate the remainder to advertising

B advertising, then what they need to spend in consumer promotion, and then allocate the remainder to trade promotion

C consumer promotion, then what they need to spend in advertising, and then allocate the remainder to trade promotion

D advertising, then what they need to spend in trade promotion, and then allocate the remainder to consumer promotion

E consumer promotion, then what they need to spend in trade promotion, and then allocate the remainder to advertising

16.5
For which of the following tasks would sales promotion probably prove **least** successful?

A encouraging repurchase of a product that did not impress consumers on first trial

B encouraging consumers to buy more of a product or buy it more frequently

C introducing a new or improved product

D capitalizing on seasonal, geographic, or special events

E encouraging consumers to 'trade up' to a larger size, a more profitable line, or another product in the line

16.6
Which of the following is **not** a benefit of sales promotions?

A they enable manufacturers to adjust to short-term variations in supply and demand

B they lead to more varied retail formats, thus giving consumers more choice

C they permit manufacturers to sell more than they normally would at the list price, thereby maintaining margins and increasing the chance to reduce unit costs through economies of scale

D they promote greater consumer awareness of value and prices

E they permanently build total category volume, benefiting large and small producers alike

16.7*
Which of the following is **not** a shortcoming of sales promotion?

A it cannot overcome problems in product pricing

B it cannot reverse a long-term sales decline

C it cannot neutralize competitive advertising or sales promotion

D it cannot compensate for inadequate levels of consumer advertising

E all of these are shortcomings

16.8
Although it is not usually favoured as a method to build consumer-franchise or brand loyalty, sales promotion may exert some positive influence if used under all of the following conditions **except**:

A when a new or established brand features a major product improvement

B when the brand is already enjoying an improving competitive trend

C when used in conjunction with a sales drive to increase shop distribution

D when used for a brand on a regular, ongoing basis

E when used in conjunction with brand advertising support

16.9
Which of the following sales-promotion tools has the intention of encouraging consumer-franchise building for a brand?

A price-off packs

B explanatory leaflet with free sample

C contests or sweepstakes

D consumer premiums

E none of these

16.10*
Which of the following is **not** usually an objective of a sales promotion campaign?

A to reach non-users

B to increase profits

C to increase product usage

D to hold current users

E to attract switchers away from competitors' brands

16.11
Which of these promotional tools is the odd one out?

A frequent-flyer plans

B trading stamps

C a rebate on the purchase of a camera

D credit card sponsored by a car manufacturer

E dividend paid by co-operatives to their members

16.12
Which of the following promotional tools are **least** effective at generating product trials?

1 refund offers (e.g. 60 pence off your next purchase)

2 on-pack premiums

3 self-liquidating premiums

4 coupons

5 sampling

A 1 and 2

B 1 and 3

C 2 and 3

D 3 and 4

E 4 and 5

16.13

The total cost to the company for running a promotional campaign is **least** predictable with which promotional tool?

A refund offers (e.g. 60 pence off your next purchase)

B on-pack premiums

C self-liquidating premiums

D coupons

E sampling

16.14*

Which of the following is **not** a characteristic of contests and sweepstakes?

A they extend and reinforce your product's image

B they are effective in building readership of your advertisements

C they are particularly useful for a product that has nothing new or exciting to say in its advertising

D they do not produce mass trial

E all of these are characteristics

16.15*

Which of the following is **not** a characteristic of sampling?

A it is the most effective and least expensive way of introducing a new product

B it is more effective than other techniques when a product's features or benefits cannot be easily communicated

C it can lack precision in reaching the best prospects

D it is best used in conjunction with other promotional tools such as advertising or personal selling

E all of these are characteristics

16.16

Which of the following is **not** a characteristic of couponing?

A the rate of redemption is greater for newspaper coupons than for either direct mail or pack-distributed coupons

B coupons are the major medium by which manufacturers offer consumers a price deal

C coupons enable the manufacturer to specify the time frame of the promotion

D coupons may give the manufacturer something with which to develop a selective demand for the brand

E all of these are characteristics

16.17

Which of the following are **not** objectives of trade promotions?

1 to build brand loyalty among retailers

2 to increase long-term sales by retailers

3 to persuade outlets to stock the brand

4 to compensate for price increases

5 to persuade outlets to push the product

A 1 and 2

B 1 and 3

C 2 and 3

D 3 and 4

E 4 and 5

16.18*

Which of the following trade promotion tools is the odd one out?

A trade shows and exhibits

B displays and point-of-purchase materials

C training materials

D manufacturer-financed in-shop demonstrations

E trade advertising

16.19

When a manufacturer offers a retailer's sales assistants rewards depending on what levels of sales each individual achieves, which trade promotion technique is being employed?

A trade incentive

B loyalty bonus

C trade contest

D push money

E trade deal

16.20

Which of the following is **not** a characteristic of co-operative advertising?

A the goal is to create consumer demand that will pull goods out of the shop

B it is particularly useful when the manufacturer has wide distribution of a product in a market

C co-operative advertising encompasses not only press advertising, but also advertising through other media

D because of parity-in-competition legislation, a co-operative advertising programme can be quite costly and difficult to control

E all of these are characteristics

16.21

Which of the following methods of evaluation is **inappropriate** for consumer sales promotion?

A comparing sales data by time period

B comparing sales data by matched markets

C comparing sales forecasts with results

D comparing sales data by retail chains/stores

E none of these

16.22*

Which of the following statements **inaccurately** describes a difficulty in focusing on sales data in the evaluation of consumer sales promotions?

A sales comparisons tend to concentrate on short-term effects, whereas analysis of the long-term effects is more appropriate

B sales analysis does not take into account the costs of the campaign

C anticipation of a sales promotion may delay purchases that would otherwise have been made, thereby biasing sales comparisons

D sales analysis does not take into account whether alternative ways of spending promotional monies would have produced better results

E it is often hard to separate the effect of the sales promotion from the effect of the overall promotional effort

Case Study 16.1
The economics of sales promotion

A manufacturer has been selling a certain style of shoe to retailers at £20 a pair. The cost of each pair is £10, and distribution and other expenses amount to £4. The manufacturer decides to offer a 10 per cent discount to the trade for a thirty-day period. About 5,000 pairs of this style are produced every month, and no unit cost savings are anticipated from greater production.

Questions 16.23–16.25 relate to this case study

16.23

What increase in sales would be required in order to maintain the manufacturer's revenue?

A 10 per cent

B 11.1 per cent

C 20 per cent

D 25 per cent

E none of these

16.24*

What increase in sales would be required in order to maintain the manufacturer's gross trading profit?

A 10 per cent

B 11.1 per cent

C 25 per cent

D 50 per cent

E none of these

16.25*

One particular shoe retailer sells an average of 20 pairs of this style each month. The usual price is £40, but the dealer has decided to pass on the manufacturer's £2 discount to the customers. The retailer calculates his overheads to be on average 35 per cent of the non-discounted retail price. What increase in sales would be required to achieve the same net profit as could be gained by taking the trade promotion but not passing it on to the customers?

A 10 per cent

B 19.4 per cent

C 25 per cent

D 33.3 per cent

E none of these

16.26*

Which theory of personal selling is based on the hierarchy of effects?

A buyer-seller similarity theory

B stimulus-response theory

C buying formula theory

D problem solution theory

E selling formula theory

16.27

Which theory of personal selling is based on obtaining a conditioned response from the prospective buyer?

A buyer-seller similarity theory

B stimulus-response theory

C buying formula theory

D   problem solution theory

E   selling formula theory

16.28*

Which theory of personal selling concentrates on customer needs on the one hand, and product features, advantages, and benefits on the other?

A   buyer-seller similarity theory

B   stimulus-response theory

C   buying formula theory

D   problem solution theory

E   selling formula theory

16.29

In a company with a marketing orientation:

A   sales activities should be considered less important than marketing activities

B   the sales manager and marketing manager should be co-equals

C   marketing and sales functions should be kept separate and distinct

D   sales are seen to be only part of the total marketing activity of the company

E   the selling budget should not exceed the marketing budget

16.30

Which of the following comparisons between personal selling and advertising are **inaccurate**?

1   personal selling is directed at the individual, whereas advertising is directed at a mass audience

2   personal selling is two-way communication, whereas advertising is one way

3   personal selling works in depth, whereas advertising works in breadth

4   personal selling exemplifies the pull effect, whereas advertising exemplifies the push effect

5   personal selling is relatively cheaper per contact, whereas advertising is relatively more expensive per contact

A   1 and 2

B   1 and 3

C   2 and 3

D   3 and 4

E   4 and 5

16.31*

Personal selling would normally be the most important component of the promotional mix for which type of goods?

A   repeat purchases of industrial goods

B   capital goods

C   consumer durables

D   fast moving consumer goods

E   it is no more important for one type of goods than another

16.32

Personal selling would normally become the most important promotional tool at which stage of the purchase process?

A   awareness

B   comprehension

C   conviction

D   purchase

E   it is no more important at one stage than at another

16.33

Which of the following is **not** a characteristic of personal selling?

A   personal selling is particularly useful in resolving doubts of undecided customers

B   feedback from personal selling is immediate and clear-cut

C   personal selling is the most adaptable communication tool in the promotional mix

D   personal selling is an effective tool for generating consumer awareness

E   all of these are characteristics

16.34*

The purpose of using a unique selling proposition (USP) in a sales presentation is to:

A   encourage the prospect to think about or investigate the product

B   commit the prospect to a position

C   reduce ambiguities and generalities to specifics

D   apply the 'hard sell'

E   reduce perceived risk

16.35*

Which of the following is **not** a characteristic of tele-marketing?

A it is impossible to overcome a buyer's objections over the telephone

B it is a very cost-effective method of prospecting sales

C it is most successful when used as an adjunct to direct mail and advertising campaigns

D it is easier for a customer to say 'no' over the telephone than if it were a face-to-face meeting

E all of these are characteristics

16.36

Which of the following functions is **not** performed by sales personnel in telemarketing?

A contacting and screening prospects

B providing technical assistance

C processing orders and arranging shipments

D assisting the field sales force

E converting inquiries into sales

16.37

Telemarketing can have an important role in all of the following situations **except**:

1 when cold canvassing has been traditionally used by the sales force

2 when the value of purchases is low

3 when the customer base is widely disbursed

4 when the product is highly technical

5 when the selling process is complex

A 1 and 2

B 1 and 3

C 2 and 3

D 3 and 4

E 4 and 5

16.38*

Building goodwill or educating the actual or potential user is the job of which type of salesperson?

A deliverer

B demand creator

C technician

D missionary

E order taker

16.39

A milkman with a domestic round exemplifies which type of salesperson?

A deliverer

B demand creator

C technician

D missionary

E order taker

16.40*

Someone selling insurance exemplifies which type of salesperson?

A deliverer

B demand creator

C technician

D missionary

E order taker

16.41

Which sales task is being performed when a salesperson chooses which present or potential customers to visit and when?

A allocating

B servicing

C information gathering

D targeting

E prospecting

16.42*

A manufacturer is clearing the warehouse of ends of ranges. One particular salesperson finds a customer who wants to buy half the available inventory, across the board. In trying to find customers for the other half, the salesperson approaches a customer who expresses a desire to buy the entire inventory, or else not place an order. Dealing with this problem is part of which sales task?

A allocating

B servicing

C information gathering

D targeting

E prospecting

16.43

When an emphasis on selling dominates a company's sales strategy, individual salespersons are likely to be assigned which of the following objectives?

1   increasing market share
2   increasing return on investment
3   achieving a certain average order size
4   increasing the average number of calls per time period
5   improving company profitability

A   1 and 2
B   1 and 3
C   2 and 3
D   3 and 4
E   4 and 5

16.44*

A large manufacturer wishes to implement a build strategy for its ladies' casual clothes business. Which salesforce strategy would be **inappropriate**?

A   offer promotional allowances and help with displays
B   sell new products to existing accounts
C   secure added distribution outlets
D   demonstrate superior new product benefits
E   offer easy credit terms

16.45

A large manufacturer wishes to implement a harvest strategy for its men's suits business. Which salesforce strategy would be **inappropriate**?

A   reduce selling costs
B   emphasize advertising support for products
C   call on large accounts
D   push volume items
E   eliminate unprofitable small accounts

16.46

A company with a relatively limited range of products would be most likely to organize its salesforce on which basis?

A   territory-product
B   market
C   product-market
D   product
E   territory

16.47

A company selling numerous unrelated technically-complex products would be most likely to organize its salesforce on which basis?

A   territory-product
B   market
C   product-market
D   product
E   territory

16.48*

A particular disadvantage of using the workload approach to determine salesforce size is that:

A   the number of sales calls is not always related to profitability
B   sales determine the selling effort with this method, whereas the selling effort should determine the sales
C   it assumes that the company's market potential and sales effectiveness are the same as its competitors
D   it is very difficult to determine the optimal size of the salesforce because of the problem of establishing a link between sales results and selling efforts
E   all of these are disadvantages

16.49

A missionary salesperson would probably put the greatest emphasis on which part of the compensation package?

A   competitions/prizes
B   fringe benefits
C   fixed amount
D   expense allowance
E   variable amount

16.50

In evaluating performance, a comparison and ranking of the sales results of various salespersons may mislead because it assumes that:

A   there are no variations in territory market potential
B   workloads are comparable
C   current sales are the only success indicator
D   competition is the same in all territories
E   all of these factors may mislead

17

DIRECT MARKETING

17.1*
The marketer's degree of control over the direct marketing process is:

A greater than for personal selling, but less than for advertising and sales promotion

B greater than for personal selling and sales promotion, but less than for advertising

C greater than for sales promotion, but less than for advertising and personal selling

D greater than for personal selling, advertising, and sales promotion

E less than for personal selling, advertising, and sales promotion

17.2
Which of the following is **not** a characteristic of direct marketing?

A it goes directly to an identified person or household

B it cannot be used in conjunction with mass media

C its goal is some type of action

D it is interactive

E it makes use of a customer or data base

17.3
Which of the following is considered to be the **least** effective use of direct marketing?

A to build awareness

B to generate sales leads

C to sample products

D to retain customer loyalty

E to win over targeted users of competitive brands

17.4*
Up to the present, for which of the following industry sectors has direct marketing played a very minor role?

A insurance

B banks and the financial sector

C retail

D travel companies

E charities

17.5
At which stage of the consumer decision-making process is direct marketing most effective?

A decision to purchase

B information gathering

C brand evaluation

D need arousal

E information processing

17.6
Which of the following would be an **inappropriate** medium for direct marketing?

A newspapers

B leaflets inserted into magazines

C outdoor advertising

D fax machine

E none of these is inappropriate

17.7*
What role does direct marketing share with personal selling?

A building company image

B establishing company rapport

C simplifying transactions

D answering customer queries

E building preferred customer relationships

17.8
Pedigree Petfoods, holding a 50 per cent share of the petfoods market in the UK, sent a mailshot to potential customers, asking them simply to describe their pet. There was no guarantee, special offer, or incentive with the letter. Pedigree followed up on the interest generated by sending personalized birthday cards, Valentines, as well as Christmas cards to regular customers. The goals of this campaign were presumably to:

1 strengthen the company's image

2 develop sales leads

3 retain customer loyalty

4 provide an incentive to buy

5 build awareness

A 1 and 2

B 1 and 3

C 2 and 3

D 3 and 4

E 4 and 5

17.9
A company deciding to use direct marketing should foresee what duration of commitment to the method?

A short-term

B medium-term

C long- or medium-term

D long-term

E indeterminate

17.10*
Which lifestyle change in the 1980s and 1990s has **not** contributed to the rapid growth of in-home buying?

A an increasing proportion of wives/partners in employment

B greater attention to leisure

C later age of marriage for men and women

D the demand for more shopping convenience

E all of these have contributed

17.11
All the following changes in the shopping environment in the 1980s and 1990s have contributed to the rapid growth of in-home buying **except:**

A higher service expectations

B greater availability and use of credit cards

C problems such as congested car parks and long queues of customers when shopping at retail outlets

D greater product line expectations

E all of these have contributed

17.12
A successful mail order business requires all of the following characteristics **except:**

1 careful inventory control

2 a well-projected distinctive benefit

3 careful management of its mailing lists

4 a very large customer base

5 lower prices than non-mail order competitors

A 1 and 2

B 1 and 3

C 2 and 3

D 3 and 4

E 4 and 5

17.13*
Mail order in the UK is distinguished by many companies offering their own credit terms, as well as accepting payment by credit card or cheque. In the USA, very few companies offer their own credit terms; payment by credit card or cheque is expected. The difference between the countries suggests that:

1 mail order goods in the UK cost relatively more than those in the USA

2 the quality of mail order merchandise is lower in the UK than in the USA

3 the socio-economic profile of mail order customers in each country may be different

4 the perceived benefit of using mail order in each country may be different

5 credit card usage is not as popular in the UK as in the USA

A 1 and 2

B 1 and 3

C 2 and 3

D 3 and 4

E 4 and 5

17.14
Which of the following is **not** usually an objective of direct mail?

A to sell a product or service

B to collect leads for the salesforce

C to communicate interesting news

D to reach a mass market

E to qualify leads for the salesforce

17.15
Which of the following is **not** an advantage of direct mail over advertising?

A   direct mail can be targeted to reach very small markets

B   with direct mail, the competition is largely unaware of when you are contacting prospects, what you are offering, and how successful you have been

C   the cost per person reached is lower for direct mail

D   direct mail enables you to measure response with far greater accuracy

E   with direct mail, expenditure is limited to those inside your target audience

17.16

From the marketing viewpoint, what is the greatest advantage of using direct mail?

A   the falling cost in computing has made this medium more attractive

B   direct mail has no geographic limitations

C   once you have gained a prospect's interest, there is nothing else to conflict with the message you put across

D   customers value its convenience for shopping

E   you can test the effectiveness of the mail message and the attractiveness of product price at relatively low cost

17.17*

A company's customer list is likely to include which of the following?

A   the frequency of purchase

B   the purchase amount

C   the type of products purchased

D   the names of other companies the customer has dealt with

E   none of these

17.18

The marketing database of a company using direct mail is likely to include all of the following information **except**:

A   the frequency of purchase

B   the purchase amount

C   the type of products purchased

D   the names of other companies the customer has dealt with

E   none of these

17.19

The selection of people for a mailing list on the basis of first name may be of use for targeting:

1   a gender group

2   an income group

3   a professional group

4   an age group

5   a social group

A   1 and 2

B   1 and 3

C   2 and 3

D   3 and 4

E   4 and 5

17.20*

A new company with a very limited promotional budget wants to send out a direct mail offer on 'house music' CDs. It approaches a few mailing-list brokers. None of them can supply a house music list, but a few have pop music lists. The company would be well advised to:

A   buy a subsample of names from a potential list, and do a test mailing to see if the response rate is high enough

B   buy a subsample of names from two or more lists, and compare test mailing results to see which has the highest response rate

C   buy an entire list from a broker, but demand a significant discount because of the loose fit

D   reject all the lists and advertise a free catalogue in selected music publications

E   reject all the lists and advertise the offer itself in selected music publications

17.21

Which variable would **not** usually be used to profile businesses for business-to-business direct mail?

A   location of business

B   type of business

C   business turnover

D   number of employees

E   all of these can be used

17.22*

A company knowing the type of customers it wishes to attract, but not having its own customer list, may decide to use selected postal codes or neighbourhood designations to target direct mail because:

A this method is cheaper than renting or buying a list from a broker

B the differences within areas are usually more important than the differences between areas

C mailing to selected areas is cheaper than mailing to everyone in the locality

D area of residence is often a good predictor of certain personal characteristics of those living there

E 20 per cent of the population is likely to account for 50 or more per cent of the purchases

17.23

A major difference in distinguishing between junk mail and direct mail is that:

A junk mail is used for unsought goods, whereas direct mail is used for goods in which the recipient has shown an interest

B junk mail usually weighs less than direct mail

C junk mail is addressed by name, whereas direct mail is usually addressed to 'the occupier'

D junk mail tends to be untargeted, whereas direct mail is targeted

E there is no difference between the two

17.24

Which of the following is **least** likely to be discarded by the recipient when it is distributed door-to-door through letterboxes?

A a free sample

B coupons

C a free entry invitation to an exhibition

D a game card

E all of these are as likely to be discarded

17.25*

Unaddressed advertising leaflets delivered street by street through letterboxes have the greatest chance of being read when:

1 some sort of benefit can be recognized instantly

2 the identity of the sender is played down

3 the design is unusual or interesting

4 there is detailed explanatory text

5 the recipient takes no notice of press or television advertising

A 1 and 2

B 1 and 3

C 2 and 3

D 3 and 4

E 4 and 5

17.26

As used by a salesforce, telemarketing probably has the greatest impact for:

A order takers

B demand creators

C missionary salespersons

D deliverers

E it has equal impact for all

17.27

Which function is the odd one out in terms of telemarketing?

A account enquiries

B complaint handling

C lead generation

D order processing

E telesales

17.28*

Which function is the odd one out in terms of telemarketing?

A test marketing

B list cleaning

C public information

D database development

E product launching

17.29*

An insurance broker advertises a free-phone telephone number in the Yellow Pages classified telephone directory, but provides only an ordinary telephone number on the stationery used for correspondence with existing clients. This disparity of treatment between prospects and existing clients suggests that the company:

1 receives many more calls from inquirers than from existing clients

2 believes it is more expensive to retain existing clients than it is to recruit new clients

3 has not adopted a thorough marketing approach for the brokerage

4 does not understand the role of inward telemarketing in customer retention

5 wants specific staff to answer new-business enquiries, and has therefore separated the two types of calls

A 1 and 2

B 1 and 3

C 2 and 3

D 3 and 4

E 4 and 5

17.30*

Advantages that telemarketing has over other forms of direct marketing are the ability to:

1 carry out test marketing

2 exploit the full range of cross-selling opportunities

3 exploit the full range of up-selling opportunities

4 reach geographically distant customers

5 target very small niche markets

A 1 and 2

B 1 and 3

C 2 and 3

D 3 and 4

E 4 and 5

17.31

Which of the following are characterized as formal, or clearly defined, applications of telemarketing?

1 sales

2 payroll handling

3 service

4 logistics

5 marketing

A 1 and 2

B 1 and 3

C 2 and 3

D 3 and 4

E 4 and 5

17.32

Informal applications of telemarketing are characterized by all of the following **except**:

A a low number of agents

B 'customers' internal to the business

C agents who are not dedicated to telephone work

D dealing with the public or external customers

E dealing with business processes

17.33

Particular advantages that telemarketing has over direct mail are:

1 fast testing

2 immediate feedback

3 two-way dialogue

4 database management

5 accurate targeting

A 1 and 2

B 1 and 3

C 2 and 3

D 3 and 4

E 4 and 5

17.34

Compared with direct mail, telebusiness:

1 has a lower volume of contacts

2 has a more consistent message

3 has higher costs per contact

4 has a lower response rate

5 is less labour intensive

A 1 and 2

B 1 and 3

C 2 and 3

D 3 and 4

E 4 and 5

17.35

Which of the following was **not** a factor in the rapid growth of telemarketing in both the USA and the UK?

A the development of premium-rate telephone services

B industry deregulation

C the falling costs of telebusiness equipment and systems

D the development of toll-free and low-tariff calls

E the increasing costs of personal sales calls

17.36

Which are usually the busiest times of the day for inbound telemarketing calls?

1 10 a.m.

2 11 a.m.

3 2 p.m.

4   3 p.m.

5   9 a.m.

A   1 and 2

B   1 and 3

C   2 and 3

D   3 and 4

E   4 and 5

17.37

Which of the following has **not** contributed to the loss of favour of the two-minute direct response television commercial?

A   production costs are high

B   it is extremely difficult to get two-minute air slots at desired times

C   it is easier to persuade people via an at-home-shopping television channel than it is through a two-minute direct response commercial

D   returns for this type of commercial historically have been poor

E   low- and medium-involvement goods have proved easier to market than high-involvement goods using this method

17.38*

The difference between multi-level or network marketing on one hand, and pyramid selling on the other is that:

A   there is no emphasis on an existing agent recruiting new agents in multi-level marketing, whereas this is a main concern in pyramid selling

B   multi-level marketing agents have defined territories, whereas pyramid-selling agents do not

C   multi-level marketing involves no investment in stock, whereas pyramid selling does

D   the organizational structure of a multi-level organization is not hierarchical, whereas it is in a pyramid-selling organization

E   there is no significant difference between them

17.39

In doorstep selling, an important difference between single-level marketing and multi-level marketing is that:

A   with single-level marketing, the agent buys goods direct from the manufacturer, whereas with multi-level marketing, the agent can buy from the manufacturer, wholesaler, or another distributor

B   with single-level marketing, the goods are usually demonstrated to a group of prospective buyers, whereas with multi-level marketing, the business is driven by the catalogue

C   with single-level marketing, agents earn commission only on their own sales, whereas in multi-level marketing, they earn commission on their own sales and the sales of others

D   single-level marketing is used primarily for relatively inexpensive goods, whereas multi-level marketing is used primarily for relatively expensive goods

E   none of these is an important difference

17.40

In cold canvassing, the person making the sales call would normally have:

A   chosen the customer or the customer's name at random

B   been referred to the customer by someone

C   previously met the person socially

D   previously sold something to the customer

E   received an inquiry from the customer

17.41*

The purpose of using response compression, whereby multiple media are utilized within a tightly defined time frame, is to:

A   generate greater incremental sales that exceed incremental costs

B   reduce the time it takes for orders to be placed

C   encourage a conditioned response when the last medium is used

D   create a high-pressure selling situation, reducing sales resistance

E   compensate for using out-of-date lists

17.42*

According to Rapp and Collins' model for 'maximarketing', using advertising to build awareness and at the same time generate a direct response is an example of which step?

A   maximized activation

B   maximized synergy

C   maximized linkage

D   maximized awareness

E   maximized sales

17.43

In 1994, the average cost of employing a telemarketing agent was about what proportion of the average cost of employing a field salesperson?

A 40 per cent

B 50 per cent

C 60 per cent

D 70 per cent

E none of these

17.44

The hardest to solve issue of public policy currently facing the direct marketing industry is:

A intrusion

B irritation

C deception

D unfairness

E invasion of privacy

17.45

Which of the following causes of returned merchandise is most likely to represent a failure in marketing?

A damage in transit

B incorrect order fulfilment

C goods not as advertised

D late arrival

E defective merchandise

17.46*

Which is the most important measure of the effectiveness of a direct mail campaign?

A the response rate

B the cost per response

C return on investment

D the cost per sale

E the conversion rate

17.47

If response to a direct mail offer is good, but the offer fails to stimulate repurchase within a year where this is an option, we can infer that:

A the list needs cleaning

B the original customers have found another source of supply

C something in the offer package has caused dissatisfaction

D follow-up mailings have been too frequent

E the goods are no longer of interest to the list members

Case Study 17.1
Measuring the effectiveness of a direct marketing campaign

China Modes has been using direct mail to sell a series of ceramic plates based on turn-of-the-century rural themes. The latest in the series is priced at £30. The order margin per unit is £15, and the selling cost is £200 per thousand. The mailing generates 20 replies per thousand letters.

China Modes' main competitor, China Discounts, has been using direct mail to sell a series of ceramic plates based on a similar theme. Its latest offering is priced at £20. The order margin per unit is £10, and the selling cost is £200 per thousand. The mailing generates 30 replies per thousand letters.

The cost of working capital is about 10 per cent.

Return on Investment is computed as follows:

$$\text{ROI} = \frac{(\text{SP} \times \text{RE}) - \text{TI}}{\text{TI}} \times 100$$

where SP = Selling Price per unit
OM = Order Margin per unit
RE = Replies per thousand
SC = Selling Cost per thousand
TI = Total Investment = ([SP - OM] x RE) + SC
ROI = Percentage Return on Investment

Questions 17.48–17.49 relate to this case study

17.48*

In order to achieve an acceptable return on investment, on its next mailing China Modes should:

A reduce the selling price in the hope of generating more replies

B improve the mailing letter in the hope of generating more replies

C try to reduce selling costs

D employ a combination of A, B, and C

E not alter anything

17.49*

If China Discount increases its selling costs to £250, and in so doing generates 40 replies per thousand letters, its return on investment would:

A increase, but be lower than China Modes' current ROI

B increase, and be the same as China Modes' current ROI

C increase, and be higher than China Modes' current ROI

D decrease, and be the same as China Modes' current ROI

E decrease, but be higher than China Modes' current ROI

17.50

As a rule of thumb, a direct marketing effort is usually considered ineffective if the sales return on investment is less than:

A 2.5 per cent

B 5 per cent

C 10 per cent

D 15 per cent

E none of these

18

SERVICES MARKETING

18.1*

In the United States in 1990, service jobs accounted for around 77 per cent of total employment, and around 70 per cent of GNP. In the United Kingdom in the early 1990s, service jobs accounted for about 67 per cent of total employment, and about 63 per cent of GDP. These figures suggest that:

A the services sector as a whole is associated with relatively low earnings

B services are now more important in the economy than they were ten years ago

C the vast majority of all new jobs in the next ten years will be in the service industry

D the highest growth areas are in non-traditional services

E none of these

18.2*

A restaurant meal represents what type of offer?

A a pure tangible good

B a tangible good with accompanying services

C a hybrid

D a service with accompanying tangible goods

E a pure service

18.3*

A flight between London and New York represents what type of offer?

A a pure tangible good

B a tangible good with accompanying services

C a hybrid

D a service with accompanying tangible goods

E a pure service

18.4

Baby-sitting represents what type of offer?

A a pure tangible good

B a tangible good with accompanying services

C a hybrid

D a service with accompanying tangible goods

E a pure service

18.5

A new car represents what type of offer?

A a pure tangible good

B a tangible good with accompanying services

C a hybrid

D a service with accompanying tangible goods

E a pure service

18.6

Physiotherapy represents what type of offer?

A a pure tangible good

B a tangible good with accompanying services

C a hybrid

D a service with accompanying tangible goods

E a pure service

18.7

The greatest amount of service would be involved with:

A a pop concert

B psychotherapy

C shoe repairs

D a bakery

E a clothes shop

18.8

The least amount of service would be involved with:

A a commuter railroad network

B a supermarket

C a telephone system

D an information desk at a DIY store

E local government

18.9*

In a hotel, the **least** amount of service would be involved with:

A   the hotel restaurant

B   the hall porter or bellboy

C   hotel reception

D   the hotel bar

E   coffee- and tea-making facilities in the room

18.10*

Which service is the odd one out?

A   car repair

B   hairdressing

C   eye testing

D   ear piercing

E   dental care

18.11

The intangibility of services is likely to lead customers to do the following **except**:

A   perceive high levels of risk

B   place great emphasis on personal information sources

C   ascribe unconnected features to the service

D   use price as a basis for assessing quality

E   experience difficulty in evaluating competing services

18.12

As a response to customer reaction to service intangibility, management may be advised to do the following **except**:

A   reduce service complexity

B   focus on service quality

C   stress tangible cues

D   seek testimonials from satisfied customers

E   all of these may be attempted

18.13*

Which of the following is **not** a characteristic of the inseparability of services?

A   services are generally first produced, then sold, and then consumed

B   consumers are often co-producers of the service

C   consumers often have to travel to the point of service production

D   service providers are often not interchangeable

E   consumers are often co-consumers of a service with others

18.14*

Which of the following **fails** to account for the problem of variability of services?

A   because of customer involvement in the process of service delivery, it can be difficult to carry out monitoring and control to insure consistent standards

B   the opportunity for pre-delivery inspection and rejection is not normally possible with services

C   people providing services differ in their health, energy, and mental set over a period of time

D   what is perceived as a good job by the service provider may not be perceived as such by the service consumer

E   all of these account for the problem

18.15

Which of the following measures would **not** normally be used to reduce the variability of service outputs?

A   careful selection and training of personnel

B   simplification of service offerings

C   widening the standards of what is acceptable

D   monitoring customer satisfaction through suggestion and complaint systems

E   standardization of the service-performance process

18.16*

Which of the following examples does **not** relate to the perishability of services?

A   'no-shows' have to pay the full fare for their seats on an airplane

B   cocktail lounges are provided for people waiting for tables at a restaurant

C   temporary staff are hired by department stores before Christmas

D   a doctor sees patients on a first-come-first-served basis

E   a hotel runs mini-break weekends

18.17

Which of the following is **not** an implication of the inability to own a service?

A   the buyer cannot determine when the service is to be carried out

B   distribution of services tends to be direct to the customer

C by buying a service, the purchaser in effect buys the right to a service process

D where intermediaries are used, they generally act as co-producer of the service

E all of these are implications

18.18*
The British School of Motoring's slogan, 'the pass masters', is appropriate because services:

A are intangible

B are inseparable

C are variable

D are perishable

E cannot be owned

18.19
Many theatres charge less for matinees than for evening performances for the same seat because services:

A are intangible

B are inseparable

C are variable

D are perishable

E cannot be owned

18.20*
Dentists in Britain often allocate a fifteen-minute appointment for a check-up, cleaning, and polish. If the patient requires further treatment (e.g. a filling), a second appointment must be made. Budgeting dentists' time in this way is done because their services:

A are intangible

B are inseparable

C are variable

D are perishable

E cannot be owned

18.21
British Rail has a television advertisement showing a young couple looking out of the train window at the passing countryside; a kindly looking old man playing chess on the train with a young boy; and a middle-aged man stretching out in his seat, with his shoes transforming into carpet slippers. A lazy tune plays in the background, inviting the listener to relax. British Rail shows these things because rail travel as a service:

A is intangible

B is inseparable

C is variable

D is perishable

E cannot be owned

18.22*
The Prudential slogan, 'I've got a piece of the Rock', with a depiction of the Rock of Gibraltar, is appropriate for insurance services because they:

A are intangible

B are inseparable

C are variable

D are perishable

E cannot be owned

18.23
Standby tickets on an airplane often cost less than those purchased well in advance of the flight because services:

A are intangible

B are inseparable

C are variable

D are perishable

E cannot be owned

18.24
A client wants his solicitor to handle certain litigation in a particular way, but the solicitor refuses on the grounds that the client's strategy, though legal, goes against her best judgment and experience. The solicitor's stand, backed up by a Code of Practice, exemplifies the point that services:

A are intangible

B are inseparable

C are variable

D are perishable

E cannot be owned

18.25
Bars often run 'happy hours' with discount drinks in the late afternoon and early evening because their services:

A are intangible

B are inseparable

C are variable

D are perishable

E cannot be owned

18.26*

The slogan of the Hotel Elysee in New York City, 'Hotel Elysee – where courtesy always prevails', is appropriate because hotel services:

A are intangible

B are inseparable

C are variable

D are perishable

E cannot be owned

18.27*

A local social security office will answer telephone inquiries only between the hours of 10 a.m. to 12 noon, and 2 p.m. to 4 p.m. because its services:

A are intangible

B are inseparable

C are variable

D are perishable

E cannot be owned

18.28*

The classification of services by the type of activity performed is **not** particularly helpful to marketers because:

1 most services are in fact a combination of services

2 the number of categories used is usually too great to deal with efficiently

3 a single production sector can cover a very diverse range of activities with quite different marketing needs

4 the categories developed have been too narrow

5 the marketing needs of a particular production-based subsector may have more in common with another unrelated subsector than with other areas within its own sector

A 1 and 2

B 1 and 3

C 2 and 3

D 3 and 4

E 4 and 5

18.29*

Which of the following statements **incorrectly** criticizes the practice of drawing a distinction between producer and consumer services?

A individuals within organizations may cause some service-buying decisions to be based on personal consumption criteria rather than simply on the service's ability to add economic benefit to the production process

B the needs of producers and consumers are the same

C a private household may act as a production unit in which services are bought not for their own intrinsic value but in order to allow some other benefit to be produced

D many services are provided simultaneously to both consumer and producer markets

E none of these is incorrect

18.30*

Customer involvement is likely to be greatest for which of the following services?

A transport of goods

B office cleaning

C operation of a bank account

D hair colouring

E carpet cleaning

18.31

Which of the following is **not** an element of the secondary service offering?

A differentiating features

B service price

C branding

D level of quality

E tangibles

18.32

For a good restaurant, which of the following features is **not** part of its secondary service offering?

A live background piano music

B fresh flowers on the table

C an ironed tablecloth

D free valet parking

E complimentary after-dinner petits fours

18.33

For a good quality hotel, which of the following features is **not** part of its secondary service offering?

A an express check out

B room service

C a television set in your room

D a fax in your room

E a complimentary bowl of fruit in your room

18.34*

Which of the following does **not** represent a problem in assessing customer service needs?

A customers desiring a service are not always consciously aware of what all their needs are

B customers often have difficulty in expressing their needs to service providers

C it is impossible to know in advance which service feature an individual will consider most important

D the need for a service is often unrecognized by the buyer until the buyer becomes aware of its availability

E customers' needs are unlikely to remain constant as the marketing environment changes

18.35

A service product audit would be expected to include the following questions **except**:

A what benefits do customers seek from the service

B what benefits are offered over and above those of the competition

C does each service provided earn sufficient financial return

D is the correct market segment being targeted

E are competitors' advantages causing the organization to lose revenue

18.36

When a higher education institution promotes its courses to new groups of mature students, this is an example of:

A market penetration

B diversification

C service development

D market extension

E market skimming

18.37

When a bank offers a new type of charge card aimed at its current customer base, this is an example of:

A market penetration

B diversification

C service development

D market extension

E market skimming

18.38*

Which service product strategy normally creates the greatest risk?

A market penetration

B diversification

C service development

D market extension

E market skimming

18.39

If a company in the service industry wishes to avoid price competition, it is best advised to:

A engage in mass advertising

B differentiate the offer, image, and delivery

C substitute sales promotion for price competition

D segment the market on the basis of lifestyle

E encourage customers to see the industry as homogeneous

18.40*

Under which conditions may a service provider be advised to consider saturation pricing for a new service?

1 when consumers have poor knowledge about prices for competing services

2 when there are no unique service features in the offering

3 when the service provider has a good record for retaining new customers

4 when the service supplier can increase prices on the basis of perceived added value on the service offering

5 when the target market is extremely price sensitive and not quality conscious

A 1 and 2

B 1 and 3

C 2 and 3

D 3 and 4

E 4 and 5

18.41

When a tour operator includes free insurance in all its package holidays, this is an example of:

A demand-based pricing

B price bundling

C price skimming

D marginal-cost pricing

E none of these

18.42

The major problem with innovations in the service industry is that:

A they are usually product-oriented rather than market-oriented

B they are expensive to introduce

C most customers are unimpressed with them

D they are easily copied

E many are too insignificant to improve service quality or increase efficiency

18.43

A service company can differentiate its service delivery through:

A people, physical environment, and process of delivery

B people, planning, and productivity

C process of delivery, performance, and profit

D people, productivity, and performance

E none of these

18.44*

Which of the following has been found to be the most important determinant of service quality?

A dependable and accurate service performance

B the physical appearance of facilities, equipment, and personnel

C the provision of caring, individualized attention

D responsiveness to customers

E ability of employees to convey trust and confidence

18.45*

A patient has strained his back to the extent that his doctor has advised complete bed rest for a week. The doctor has visited the patient twice to show care, but the patient interprets this as an indication that something is seriously wrong. This anxiety is a result of a gap between:

A service-quality specifications and service delivery

B perceived service and expected service

C consumer expectation and management perception

D service delivery and external communications

E management perception and service-quality specification

18.46*

While the student to staff ratio has been rising, British universities have been under pressure from the state funding authorities to improve the quality of teaching and increase research output from staff. There has been considerable difficulty in achieving both of these aims simultaneously. In many institutions, the situation has led to staff dissatisfaction and lower morale because of the gap between:

A service-quality specifications and service delivery

B perceived service and expected service

C consumer expectation and management perception

D service delivery and external communications

E management perception and service-quality specification

18.47

Which of the following would **not** be a device to measure service performance?

A comparison shopping

B customer surveys

C suggestion and complaint forms

D ghost shopping/test purchasing

E all of these can be used

18.48

Which of the following measures is **least** likely to lead to an improvement in service productivity?

A introducing a staff bonus scheme based on customer recommendation

B increasing service quantity by surrendering some quality

C industrializing the service by adding equipment and standardizing the product

D sending service providers on a skill-improvement courses

E presenting customers with incentives to substitute their own for company labour

18.49*

Which of the following statements **incorrectly** characterizes customer dissatisfaction?

A a satisfied customer tells three people about a good product, but a dissatisfied customer will complain to eleven people

B customers who are most upset tend to be the company's best customers

C in rectifying a complaint, the first requirement is for those receiving complaints to be well-trained and empowered to resolve problems speedily and satisfactorily

D customers are dissatisfied with their purchases about 25 per cent of the time

E none of these is incorrect

18.50

Which of the following statements **incorrectly** characterizes product support services?

A firms providing a high-quality product support service can charge more, grow faster, and make more profits than less service-oriented competitors

B customers are most concerned about an interruption of the service they expect from the product

C product support service is becoming a major battleground for competitive advantage

D a key to successful service strategy is to design products so that they rarely break down and, if they do, are easily and rapidly fixed with minimal service expense

E the importance attached to a product's reliability, the seller's service dependability, and the cost of regular maintenance and repair is consistent among different products and product users

19

INTERNATIONAL MARKETING

19.1*
International marketing includes all of the following activities **except**:

A exporting

B buying stocks and shares in foreign companies

C importing

D countertrade

E overseas manufacturing

19.2
Which of the following is the **least** advisable reason for a company to engage in international marketing?

A to reduce dependence on any one market so as to reduce risk

B to expand domestic capacity in the hope that domestic demand will eventually improve

C to take advantage of higher profit opportunities in foreign markets

D to continue to service current customers who are going abroad

E all of these are equally as advisable

19.3
The theory of comparative advantage in international trade suggests that:

A countries that develop and produce a product first tend to have a permanent advantage over later producers

B a country tends to produce and export those goods in which it has the greater comparative advantage, and import those goods in which it has the least comparative advantage

C the greater the labour productivity for an individual product, the greater that country's comparative advantage over its rivals in protecting the domestic market and generating exports

D countries with large domestic or captive markets tend to have a great comparative advantage over countries with only small domestic markets

E none of these

19.4
An American tobacco company selling cigarette-making knowledge to China would be an example of using international marketing to:

A use up excess production capacity

B take advantage of a low-cost position due to experience curve economies

C counterattack foreign competitors in their own markets

D respond to lagging product cycles in developing countries

E none of these

19.5*
Important characteristics of a company with a global, rather than an international, perspective are that it:

1 concentrates on product markets rather than geographic markets

2 adopts a different marketing mix for each country

3 treats the world as the market, with individual countries as submarkets

4 uses large regional areas, rather than individual countries, to segment the market

5 insists on using an internationally-sourced range of materials or components in its products

A 1 and 2

B 1 and 3

C 2 and 3

D 3 and 4

E 4 and 5

19.6*
An organization with a global perspective tries to:

A develop a different product for each country

B segment the world on the basis of language groupings

C find out to what extent shared customer needs exist in different countries

D   use an undifferentiated marketing strategy within foreign countries

E   minimize experience curve effects

19.7
Marketing has the greatest role to play in overcoming which of the following difficulties in entering and competing in foreign markets?

A   foreign exchange problems

B   problems of product and communication adaptation

C   technological pirating

D   tariffs

E   bribery and corruption

19.8*
Which phase in the production and trade cycle is comparable to the maturity stage of the product life cycle?

A   when the innovator starts to export to a foreign country

B   when the innovator commences foreign production

C   when foreign producers begin to export to third-country markets

D   when foreign producers start exporting to the innovator's home country

E   none of these phases is comparable

19.9*
At which phase(s) in the production and trade cycle for a given product would we expect exports from the innovating country to decrease?

A   when the innovator commences foreign production

B   when foreign producers begin to export to third-country markets

C   when foreign producers start exporting to the innovator's home country

D   at phases B and C

E   at phases A, B, and C

19.10
Which of the following measures by a foreign country would be most likely to encourage exporters to that country to try to export more expensive products with higher margins?

A   a tariff levied on quantity

B   exchange control

C   a tariff based on the value of the goods

D   a quota, or quantitative restriction

E   invisible trade barriers

19.11
A company is best advised to operate only in a few, rather than many, countries when:

A   market entry and market control costs are high

B   it wants a deep commitment and penetration in each market

C   dominant foreign firms can establish high barriers to entry

D   product and communication adaptation costs are high

E   in all of these cases

19.12
Which of the following is usually **not** a criterion for deciding on the type of country to consider for international marketing efforts?

A   the number and size of competitors

B   whether the country fits in with the company mission and business philosophy

C   geographic location

D   level of economic development

E   political and legal systems

19.13*
Once the type of country has been determined, the **least** important selection criteria in choosing which particular country or countries to enter are:

1   cultural similarity

2   market attractiveness

3   infrastructure

4   risk level

5   competitive advantage

A   1 and 2

B   1 and 3

C   2 and 3

D   3 and 4

E   4 and 5

19.14*
Once the company has initially ranked countries it may wish to enter, its next step is to:

A   determine what marketing mix to use

B   gain the various licences and permits to operate

C insure that the channels of distribution are adequate

D estimate the rate of return on investment

E make a pilot export delivery

19.15

Which of the following statements **incorrectly** criticizes the use of per capita income measurements to determine market attractiveness?

A per capita income figures are meaningful only when the distribution of income within the country is skewed, which is uncommon

B the sales of many goods show little correlation with per capita income

C devaluation or revaluation of a currency can change per capita income without changing demand for any given product

D per capita income comparisons between countries are realistic only if the exchange rates reflect the relative domestic purchasing power of the various currencies, which cannot be assumed

E none of these is correct

19.16

The attempt to sell packet cake mixes in Japan, when most Japanese homes do not have ovens, or milk powder for babies in countries that lack pure water supply and bottle sterilization facilities, are examples of:

A ethnocentrism

B imperialism

C regionalism

D polycentrism

E geocentrism

19.17

Which of the following is **inappropriate** as an international marketing strategy for a company?

A becoming the lowest-cost producer, and competing on the basis of low prices

B offering internationally only those parts of its product or service portfolio that have unquestionable competitive advantages

C avoiding competition, and seeking government help to operate in protected markets

D providing a differentiated product, and competing on the basis of providing unique value to the customer

E none of these is inappropriate

19.18

Which of the following does **not** constitute a possible source of competitive advantage in a firm's value-added chain?

A a firm's proprietary technology

B a firm's superior manufacturing

C a firm's skills in marketing

D the international product life cycle

E all of these are possible sources

19.19

Which of the following is **inappropriate** as a company's goal for a product line within a particular country market?

A achieving a certain market share

B challenging strong global competitors as a means of preserving competitive balance between countries

C establishing a market presence

D achieving a profit target

E none of these is inappropriate

19.20*

A company is well advised to individualize the marketing mix it uses for each foreign market when:

1 the product is politically sensitive

2 the product is at the same stage of the PLC in all of the markets involved

3 the product has highly emotional associations

4 the foreign markets are geographically similar

5 capital requirements are high

A 1 and 2

B 1 and 3

C 2 and 3

D 3 and 4

E 4 and 5

19.21*

A company is well advised to standardize the marketing mix it uses for foreign markets when:

1 the markets share a similar culture

2 research and development costs for a product are high

3 corporate leadership shows high flexibility

4 the markets are not price sensitive

5 the markets show resistance to change

A 1 and 2

B 1 and 3

C 2 and 3

D 3 and 4

E 4 and 5

19.22

The attempt to see how far a brand can be stretched across national and regional boundaries to maximize economies of scale reflects a:

A product orientation

B market orientation

C production orientation

D sales orientation

E societal-market orientation

19.23*

Which of the following situations is the odd one out?

A certain American films have been banned or heavily cut in Great Britain because the authorities believed they were too violent

B Parker changed its advertising for ballpoint pens in Latin America because the word 'bola' meant 'ball' in some countries but, 'revolution' or 'lie' in others

C Philips had to reduce the size of its electric shavers to fit the smaller Japanese hands

D countries where women's major role is defined as homemaking are more likely to have consumer prices set by bargaining

E in Asian and Arabic countries, ties to suppliers and buyers are often based on kinship, so that non-family members may be excluded from business transactions within a specific channel of distribution

19.24*

Which of the following would **not** be a possible marketing implication of selling a relatively complex product, requiring written instructions, in a country with widespread illiteracy?

A the instructions and package label may have to be adapted

B if girls and women are largely excluded from formal education, marketing programmes must differ from those aimed at the Western-style home-maker

C the product may have to be modified

D a mass-marketing strategy would probably be more effective than a niche-marketing strategy

E it would be better to concentrate on the urban population

19.25

The method of entering foreign markets that requires the **least** amount of commitment is:

A indirect exporting

B wholly-owned foreign production

C licensing

D direct exporting

E joint ventures

19.26

The method of entering foreign markets that requires the **greatest** amount of commitment is:

A indirect exporting

B wholly-owned foreign production

C licensing

D direct exporting

E joint ventures

19.27

The method of entering foreign markets that involves the **most** control is:

A indirect exporting

B wholly-owned foreign production

C licensing

D direct exporting

E joint ventures

19.28*

All of the following are advantages of indirect export over direct export **except**:

A the firm does not have to develop an overseas sales-force

B indirect export involves less risk

C the firm does not have to set up an export department

D fewer product adaptations are required

E the exporter needs no set of foreign contacts

19.29

A middleman who agrees to manage a company's export activities is called:

A a dependent middleman

B a domestic-based export merchant

C a co-operative organization

D a domestic-based export agent

E an export-management company

19.30

Trading companies are examples of which type of middlemen?

A a dependent middleman

B a domestic-based export merchant

C a co-operative organization

D a domestic-based export agent

E an export-management company

19.31

Which of the following is **not** an advantage of using licensing to become involved with international marketing?

A the licensor gains entry into the foreign market at little risk

B the licensee gains production expertise or a well-known product without having to start from the very beginning

C even a company with no investment capital can enter a foreign market

D many governments favour licensing over direct investment

E the licensor has more control over the licensee than if it had set up its own production facilities

19.32

Which of the following is **not** a strategic benefit of choosing joint ventures rather than starting wholly-owned manufacturing abroad?

A a foreign firm can quickly obtain local marketing skills and contacts

B in industries characterized by a small number of competitors, the foreign firm may find entry barriers too high for solo entry into a market

C the foreign firm can benefit from a ready-established distribution network

D there is less danger of expropriation with a joint venture

E all of these are strategic benefits

19.33*

Contract manufacturing abroad is **inadvisable** when:

A the firm abroad cannot undertake marketing functions

B profits from marketing activities are small

C the firm going abroad is unsure whether the market is large enough

D foreign investment is not feasible for the firm going abroad

E none of these conditions make contract manufacturing abroad inadvisable

19.34

Building its own manufacturing facilities abroad may be more beneficial than acquiring a foreign company when:

A the firm is interested in entering the market quickly

B the firm wants to use the foreign base as a springboard to enter a regional economic grouping

C the investor cannot envisage synergies with a foreign company

D there is a shortage of qualified labour

E the management of the firm abroad is weak

19.35

When a company decides to introduce a product into a foreign market without any change, it is using which adaptation strategy?

A product invention

B dual adaptation

C straight extension

D product adaptation

E communication adaptation

19.36

When an American film distributed in France has the dialogue dubbed into French, this is an example of which adaptation strategy?

A product invention

B dual adaptation

C straight extension

D product adaptation

E communication adaptation

19.37*

When a company reintroduces a previously deleted product into a new foreign market, it is using which adaptation strategy?

A product invention

B dual adaptation

C straight extension

D product adaptation

E communication adaptation

19.38

A straight extension strategy for a foreign market is likely to be **least** effective for which of these products?

A after shave lotion

B cameras

C video cassette recorders

D cordless hand drills

E transistor radios

19.39*

Building a global brand:

1 is inherent in using a standardized product

2 depends on a growing divergence of consumer tastes for its success

3 may be advantageous in securing access to distribution channels

4 translates into the highest market share

5 is hindered by linguistic differences among the various markets

A 1 and 2

B 1 and 3

C 2 and 3

D 3 and 4

E 4 and 5

19.40*

All of the following factors may encourage standardization of international warranties **except**:

A international companies are unlikely to accept different warranties on the same products, they buy in different places

B products bought in one market but used in another should logically have uniform warranties

C on products that can affect human safety, warranties throughout the world should be uniform because

the need of users is the same all over the world

D if a company with a worldwide service programme has just one production source for world markets, one would expect a uniform warranty

E economies of scale could be achieved if companies directed their attention toward warranty standardization

19.41

Poor countries may require more expensive packaging in spite of their lower purchasing power:

1 because the size of the packages is usually bigger in poor countries

2 because of local cultural factors

3 because of long, slow distribution channels

4 because of poor transportation and storage conditions

5 because the packaging is re-used for storage and other purposes

A 1 and 2

B 1 and 3

C 2 and 3

D 3 and 4

E 4 and 5

19.42

The use of a single international advertising agency by companies selling relatively standardized products is likely to produce all the following benefits **except**:

A yielding cost savings

B increasing the creativity of the advertising campaign

C improving corporate awareness

D co-ordinating the advertising in all markets

E achieving a similarity of appeals worldwide

19.43*

Since regulations on sales promotion vary from country to country, international companies generally:

A try to develop sales promotions that can be used everywhere

B assign sales promotion as a responsibility of local management

C concentrate on straight price reductions

D avoid using sales promotions

E concentrate on sales displays

19.44

In 1992, the price of certain new British-made cars was as much as 44 per cent more in Britain than in the cheapest European Community country. This discrepancy encouraged some individuals and import firms to buy cars in Europe and import them into the UK. Which of the following statements **incorrectly** characterizes such gray marketing?

A established distributors lose motivation to sell the products as they see their margins eroded

B manufacturers may ultimately lose markets because the gray marketer competes only on price and drives away customers who seek after-sales service or other forms of support

C the operation of gray markets provides manufacturers with an outlet for excess production and may also allow a firm to gain economies of scale

D gray marketing arises because of unsustainable price differences between two markets

E none of these statements is incorrect

19.45*

An export price may be lower than the home market price but, nevertheless, be more profitable to the manufacturer because:

1 the domestic distribution system may be less efficient than one abroad

2 some costs allocated to domestic sales do not apply to export sales

3 the lower income levels in some foreign markets may require the firm to set a lower price to achieve sales

4 foreign competition may dictate a lower price

5 the firm has dumped the product abroad

A 1 and 2

B 1 and 3

C 2 and 3

D 3 and 4

E 4 and 5

19.46*

Which of the following statements **incorrectly** characterizes the operation of transfer pricing in international markets?

A the products may be transferred at artificially low prices into a country where an early devaluation is thought to be a probability

B products may be transferred at high prices into a country affected by high inflation rates

C products may be transferred at high prices into a country from which dividend repatriation is restricted or subject to government taxes

D products may be transferred into high tax countries at high transfer prices so that the profits in the high tax country are virtually eliminated

E products may be transferred into high duty countries at an artificially low transfer price so that value-based duty paid will be low

19.47

The expansion of large-scale retailing in many developing countries is particularly hampered by:

A the long channels of distribution

B the custom of price haggling

C high markups

D government restriction

E all of these

19.48

Which of the following characteristics is **not necessarily** required for a firm to follow a global high-share strategy?

A all functional areas should make maximum use of economies of scale and accumulated experience

B the firm must have achieved a large market share and a high degree of product standardization

C the firm's operations and its image must be global

D the firm should be a technological pioneer

E all of these are necessarily required

19.49

Which of the following characteristics is **not necessarily** required for a firm to follow a global niche strategy?

A the focus is on a product that is relatively insensitive to price competition

B the niche is of negligible interest to major competitors

C the firm relies on national barriers to entry

D the firm caters to special market needs

E the firm can defend itself against an attacking major competitor through the customer goodwill it has built up

19.50*

Which competitive market strategy is a company adopting when it chooses geographic areas in which major competitors are weak or non-existent, and offers products that are similar to those that competitors sell in comparable product markets elsewhere?

A   frontal attack

B   flanking

C   local high-share strategy

D   market encirclement

E   product bypassing

20

MARKETING RESEARCH

20.1
After determining the research design, the next step in the research process is to:

A collect the data

B design the data collection method and forms

C formulate the problem

D decide on sample size

E prepare the research proposal

20.2
The sampling frame relates to:

A how the information will be gathered from the sample

B the form of the sample

C the size of the sample

D the list of population elements from which the sample will be selected

E all of these

20.3
The research problem should be clearly defined so that:

A good communication exists between the researcher and the decision-maker

B the research itself can be designed properly

C the researcher knows what results to expect

D the decision-maker understands the decision to be made

E the respondents are able to understand it in its entirety

20.4
Which of the following factors is inappropriate to consider when designing a marketing research project?

A the decision-maker's environment

B the corporate culture

C the consequences of alternative actions

D the objectives of the decision-maker

E none of these should affect the design

20.5
The sample design stage of the research process includes specifying:

A the population from which the sample elements will be drawn

B the sampling frame

C the form of the sample

D the sample size

E all of these

20.6*
Which of the following is **not** part of the data analysis and interpretation stage of the research process?

A assignment of numerals to the observations

B application of a test of statistical significance

C collection of the data

D classifications and cross-classifications that result from counting the observations

E they are all part of this stage

20.7*
Which of the following steps should **not** be used in designing a specific research project?

A determining the sample size

B listing secondary outcome probabilities

C specifying research objectives

D organizing fieldwork

E selecting a sample type

20.8*
Which of the following statements correctly characterizes Bayes' Rule?

A it plays an important role in determining the expected value under uncertainty

B it provides a formal mechanism for revising initial probabilities in the light of additional information

C it is too subjective in its application to be used in marketing research

D it provides a scheme for easily calculating expected value

E it plays an important role in determining the expected value of perfect information

20.9

Using different advertisements in different geographic areas, and determining which advertisement was associated with the greatest increase in sales is an example of:

A causal research

B exploratory research

C experimental research

D descriptive research

E heuristic research

20.10*

A marketing research study is using three focus groups, each consisting of eight randomly chosen consumers, to discuss average monthly purchases of a particular brand. The research design can be criticized on the grounds that:

1 the same results may not be obtained by other researchers at other times

2 there are too few members in the groups

3 there are too few groups

4 individuals for focus groups should be selected on a quota basis

5 focus groups are inappropriate for quantitative research

A 1 and 2

B 1 and 3

C 2 and 3

D 3 and 4

E 4 and 5

20.11

It is **inappropriate** to use an exploratory study to:

1 discuss ideas and insights

2 formulate a problem for more precise investigation

3 determine cause and effect relationships

4 describe the characteristics of certain groups

5 establish priorities for future research

A 1 and 2

B 1 and 3

C 2 and 3

D 3 and 4

E 4 and 5

20.12

Which of the following is capable of providing more convincing evidence of causal relationships?

A an exploratory design

B a descriptive design

C an experiment

D turnover analysis

E cross-sectional analysis

20.13*

You have been asked to find out why the market share of a particular ice cream has declined in the last two quarters. The most appropriate research strategy would be:

A a descriptive study involving a field survey of actual and potential customers

B an experimental study

C an exploratory study

D a field experiment followed by an exploratory study

E an experimental study followed by a descriptive study

20.14

According to the data in Table 20.1, how many families in the panel switched toothpaste brands between December 1993 and December 1994?

A 50

B 445

C 555

D insufficient information for calculation

E none of these

20.15*

According to the data in Table 20.1, the brand with a brand loyalty probability of 0.5 is:

A A

B B

C C

D D

E E

Table 20.1
Toothpaste purchases by panel families in 1993 and 1994

Number of families purchasing a brand in December 1993

	Brand	A	B	C	D	E	Total
	A	170	50	40	30	10	300
Number of families	B	60	100	20	20	10	210
purchasing a brand in	C	15	10	90	20	30	165
December 1994	D	30	20	15	130	0	195
	E	25	20	10	10	65	130
	Total	300	200	175	210	115	1000

20.16*

When using the time order of occurrence of variables as evidence of a causal relationship between two variables:

1 a relationship between the two variables can be proved

2 the occurrence of a causal factor may follow the occurrence of the event

3 the occurrence of a causal factor may precede the occurrence of the event

4 the occurrence of a causal factor may be simultaneous with the occurrence of the event

5 it is necessary to exclude the possibility that one term in the relationship could be both a 'cause' and an 'effect' of the other term

A 1 and 2

B 1 and 3

C 2 and 3

D 3 and 4

E 4 and 5

20.17

Which of the following research designs introduce selection bias?

1 views on the question of safe sex are compared for those who did, and those who did not, read a certain report on AIDS

2 views on European Community agricultural policy are compared for six Italians selected at random in the centre of Rome and six Italians selected at random in the centre of Naples

3 a product is advertised only in Boston, and five department stores in Boston are matched with five in New York to determine the effect of the advertising on sales

4 the sixteen hotels of a national chain are randomly divided into two equal groups; the corporate colour scheme in the foyer is changed for one group; customer reaction to the initial welcome is tested between groups

5 all the students taking a university course are asked to evaluate the lecturer at the end of the semester, and the results are compared from year to year

A 1 and 2

B 1 and 3

C 2 and 3

D 3 and 4

E 4 and 5

20.18

A single group of respondents is exposed to an experimental variable and then observed once for their response. This type of study is called a:

A one-shot case study

B a static group comparison

C a one-group pre-test/post-test study

D a longitudinal study

E a post experimental study

20.19

Which of the following statements **incorrectly** characterizes the differences between primary and secondary data?

A primary data are gathered for the immediate study at hand, whereas secondary data are not

B a study should be started by gathering primary data, with secondary data being used only to fill the gaps

C it is usually more costly to acquire primary data than secondary data

D primary data are usually far more accurate than secondary data

E it is possible to achieve great time economies by using secondary data

20.20*

When unstructured-undisguised questionnaires are used, the purpose of the study is:

A open-ended

B to define the responses which are open-ended

C not communicated to the respondents

D clear, but the responses to the questions are dichotomous

E clear, but the responses to the questions are open ended.

20.21

In designing a questionnaire, the appropriate first step is to:

A determine the type of questions and method of administration

B determine the content of individual questions

C determine the wording of each question

D specify what information is being sought

E determine the form of response to each question

20.22*

When a respondent is asked to indicate the amount of agreement/disagreement with a statement, the research is using which methodology?

A multiple choice

B Likert scale

C semantic differential

D rating scale

E importance scale

20.23*

When a respondent is asked to select a point between two bipolar words to represent the direction and intensity of his or her feelings, the research is using which methodology?

A multiple choice

B Likert scale

C semantic differential

D rating scale

E importance scale

20.24*

Which shortcoming of the method of equal-appearing intervals is overcome by using the method of summated ratings?

A the subjects' inability to express the intensity of feeling with an equal-appearing interval scale

B the difficulties encountered in developing a large number of statements

C the costs due to the size of the judgement sample required with equal-appearing intervals

D the subjective nature of item analysis with the method of equal-appearing intervals

E the difficulty of generating scores for subjects

20.25

The ordinal scale represents a higher level of measurement than the nominal scale because:

A it has a natural zero

B the magnitude of the differentials is shown

C the assigned numerals serve to identify the objects

D it has an arbitrary zero

E the assigned numerals represent the order as well as identifying the object

20.26

Multidimensional scaling is concerned with:

A the mapping and transformation of distances

B the spatial relationship of objective data

C mapping perceptions and preferences

D mapping the relationship between a dependent variable and two or more independent variables

E evaluating the positive and negative aspects of an object

20.27*

Which of the following are probability samples?

1 convenience sample

2 cluster sample

3 stratified random sample

4 quota sample

A 1 and 2

B 1 and 3

C 2 and 3

D 1 and 4

E 3 and 4

20.28*
Which of the following are non-probability samples?

1 convenience sample
2 cluster sample
3 stratified random sample
4 quota sample

A 1 and 2
B 1 and 3
C 2 and 3
D 1 and 4
E 3 and 4

20.29
When every member of the population has a known equal chance of selection, which sampling methodology is being used?

A judgement sample
B cluster sample
C simple random sample
D quota sample
E convenience sample

20.30
When the researcher finds and interviews a prescribed number of people in each of several categories, which sampling methodology is being used?

A judgement sample
B cluster sample
C simple random sample
D quota sample
E convenience sample

20.31
A sample which relies on the researcher's ability to locate an initial set of respondents with desired characteristics, who then identify other suitable people, is an example of a:

A judgement sample
B cluster sample
C simple random sample
D quota sample
E convenience sample

20.32
The sampling distribution of a statistic refers to:

A the distribution of the variable in the parent population
B the distribution of all possible sample values of the statistic which could be drawn from the parent population under the specified sampling plan
C the unbiased nature of most sample statistics
D the distribution of the variable in a particular sample
E the spread of the variable in the parent population

Case Study 20.1
Estimating sample size

A researcher wishes to know the average annual amount women in a certain area spend on casual clothes. Historically, the variation in expenditure has been £100.

Questions 20.33–20.35 relate to this case study

20.33*
If the researcher wants to be 95 per cent confident that the estimated expenditure will be within £25 of the true population value, the required sample size (use $z = 2$) should be:

A 10
B 75
C 100
D 250
E none of these

20.34*
If the researcher wants to increase the confidence level from 95 per cent to 99 per cent, what will be the effect on required sample size?

A the ratio of the new sample size to the old is 9/4
B the ratio of the new sample size to the old is 4/9
C the sample size will decrease in proportion to the increase in the confidence level
D the ratio of the new sample size to the old is 3/2
E the ratio of the new sample size to the old is 2/3

20.35*
If the researcher did not know the population variance but estimated that the lower limit of expenditure would be £75 and the upper limit £975, the best estimate of the standard deviation would be:

A £75
B £100

C £150

D £525

E none of these

20.36
The relationship between sampling errors, non-sampling errors, and sample size is such that as sample size increases:

A sampling errors will increase while non-sampling errors decrease

B sampling errors will increase while non-sampling errors remain the same

C sampling errors will remain the same while non-sampling errors may even increase

D sampling errors will decrease while non-sampling errors remain the same

E sampling errors will decrease while non-sampling errors may even increase

20.37
Which one of the following is basically a sampling frame problem?

A non-coverage errors

B observation errors

C no one at home

D refusals

E designated respondents not at home when the interviewer calls

20.38
The main way to control for potential bias through the interviewer's attitudes, opinions, and perceptions is by:

A matching the backgrounds of interviewer and interviewee

B comparing the interviewer's responses to the questionnaire with those of the interviewees

C recruiting interviewers with similar socio-economic background

D training the interviewer

E insuring that the interviewer follows a rigid set of procedures while conducting the survey

20.39*
The *t*-test is **inappropriate** for investigating the difference in two sample means when:

A the variance in the two populations can be assumed to be equal

B the characteristic of interest is normally distributed in each population

C the data are ordinal or nominally scaled

D the samples are independent

E a pooled estimate for the overall variance is called for

20.40
Analysis of the relationship of a set of variables among themselves relates to analysis of:

A predictor variables

B dependence

C consequent variables

D interdependence

E independence

20.41
In the statistical test of an hypothesis, which of the following statements are **incorrect**?

1 if you cannot reject the null hypothesis, you must accept it as valid

2 the power associated with a statistical test is the probability of incorrectly rejecting a false null hypothesis

3 a Type II error consists of accepting the null hypothesis when it is false

4 if you reject the null hypothesis, you must accept the alternate hypothesis

5 a Type I error consists of not rejecting the null hypothesis when it is false

A 1 and 2

B 1 and 3

C 2 and 3

D 3 and 4

E 4 and 5

20.42
If you wanted to investigate the relationship among all the variables considered at once, the most appropriate analytical technique would be:

A factor analysis

B multiple regression analysis

C cluster analysis

D linear discriminant analysis

E conjoint measurement

20.43

The chi-square test is appropriate in situations where:

A the subjects are matched

B frequencies are unimportant

C more than two related samples are being compared

D the researcher is interested in all classes of the variable and does not wish to dichotomize it

E the trials are independent

20.44

If a marketer were interested in whether purchasers and non-purchasers of a certain product were equally divided into low, medium, and high income groups, the appropriate statistical test to use would be:

A analysis of variance

B the Kolmogorov-Smirnov test

C chi-square

D the z-test for difference in two means

E paired difference t-test

20.45

A multiple choice examination has been used for three consecutive years under the usual security procedures, which include prohibiting students from removing the examination papers and their notes from the examination room at the conclusion of the exam. The professor decides to compare the examination results to see if there has been any 'leakage' of questions from year to year. Which statistical test should be used?

A analysis of variance

B the Kolmogorov-Smirnov test

C chi-square

D the z-test for difference in two means

E paired difference t-test

20.46*

Which of the following statements about multiple regression analysis is **incorrect**?

A multiple regression analysis depends on the independent variables being correlated with each other

B the magnitude of the regression co-efficients associated with the various independent variables can be compared directly only if they are scaled in the same units or if the data have been standardized

C regression analysis is useful in determining whether variables are associated with each other

D regression analysis cannot prove causation

E as a rule of thumb, the sample size for multiple regression analysis should be equal to at least ten to fifteen times the number of predictor variables

20.47*

If the correlation between variables x and y is equal to 0.80, which of the following statements is correct?

A x and y are highly related, whereby a positive change in x is accompanied by a positive change in y

B the two variables x and y are not related to each other

C the coefficient of determination is equal to 0.64

D x and y are highly related, whereby a negative change in x is accompanied by a positive change in y

E x and y are highly related, whereby a negative change in x is accompanied by a positive change in y

20.48

Discriminant analysis would be **inappropriate** for the statistical analysis of data collected to answer which of the following questions?

A how do consumers who show a high probability of purchasing a new product differ in demographic characteristics from consumers with a low purchase probability?

B how do consumers who purchase various brands differ from those who do not?

C of the five new shades of blue house paint a manufacturer has developed, do consumers have a preference for one particular shade?

D how do consumers who frequently visit one particular restaurant differ from those who frequently visit another?

E do consumers who have taken out personal accident insurance differ in life-style from those who have not?

20.49

The major purposes of factor analysis are:

1 to compare dependent with independent variables

2 to indicate on which observed variables entities differ most

3 to minimize the chance of making Type I or Type II errors

4 to identify the dimensions that underlie constructs

5 to summarize the important information in a set of variables by a new smaller set of variables

A 1 and 2

B 1 and 3

C 2 and 3

D 3 and 4

E 4 and 5

20.50

Cluster analysis is **inappropriate** for which of the following applications?

A determining the underlying dimensions of customer satisfaction

B grouping customers according to perceived product benefits

C determining spheres of opinion leadership

D assessing the similarity of world markets

E undertaking life-style segmentation

SUGGESTED ANSWERS

1 MARKETING STRATEGY

1.1	B	1.13	E	1.26	B	1.38	C
1.2	A	1.14	D	1.27	C	1.39	B
1.3	C	1.16	A	1.28	B	1.41	E
1.4	E	1.17	E	1.29	D	1.42	C
1.6	E	1.18	D	1.31	E	1.43	A
1.7	B	1.19	D	1.32	B	1.44	C
1.8	B	1.21	C	1.33	B	1.46	D
1.9	B	1.22	B	1.34	A	1.47	A
1.11	C	1.23	E	1.36	A	1.48	D
1.12	D	1.24	D	1.37	C	1.49	C

2 SEGMENTATION AND POSITIONING

2.1	E	2.13	B	2.26	A	2.38	E
2.2	C	2.14	B	2.27	C	2.39	B
2.3	A	2.16	B	2.28	D	2.41	D
2.4	C	2.17	E	2.29	B	2.42	B
2.6	D	2.18	D	2.31	C	2.43	E
2.7	B	2.19	A	2.32	C	2.44	C
2.8	D	2.21	D	2.33	E	2.46	D
2.9	E	2.22	E	2.34	C	2.47	A
2.11	D	2.23	E	2.36	E	2.48	E
2.12	C	2.24	C	2.37	D	2.49	C

3 CONSUMER BEHAVIOUR

3.1	E	3.13	A	3.26	A	3.38	E
3.2	C	3.14	A	3.27	E	3.39	D
3.3	A	3.16	B	3.28	B	3.41	D
3.4	C	3.17	C	3.29	E	3.42	A
3.6	E	3.18	D	3.31	A	3.43	B
3.7	B	3.19	A	3.32	D	3.44	A
3.8	C	3.21	B	3.33	D	3.46	C
3.9	A	3.22	E	3.34	B	3.47	C
3.11	C	3.23	E	3.36	C	3.48	D
3.12	C	3.24	E	3.37	D	3.49	E

4 INDUSTRIAL AND ORGANIZATIONAL MARKETING

4.1	D	4.13	D	4.26	B	4.38	B
4.2	B	4.14	D	4.27	A	4.39	D
4.3	A	4.16	E	4.28	C	4.41	A
4.4	C	4.17	E	4.29	E	4.42	D
4.6	C	4.18	A	4.31	A	4.43	A
4.7	E	4.19	E	4.32	B	4.44	A
4.8	B	4.21	E	4.33	B	4.46	C
4.9	D	4.22	D	4.34	D	4.47	C
4.11	E	4.23	D	4.36	C	4.48	D
4.12	E	4.24	A	4.37	D	4.49	E

5 COMPETITIVE MARKETING STRATEGY

5.1	E	5.13	C	5.26	B	5.38	B
5.2	C	5.14	B	5.27	C	5.39	D
5.3	A	5.16	B	5.28	D	5.41	C
5.4	D	5.17	E	5.29	C	5.42	C
5.6	B	5.18	A	5.31	B	5.43	D
5.7	C	5.19	A	5.32	B	5.44	E
5.8	D	5.21	E	5.33	B	5.46	B
5.9	C	5.22	D	5.34	C	5.47	B
5.11	D	5.23	A	5.36	A	5.48	D
5.12	C	5.24	E	5.37	B	5.49	C

6 PRODUCTS AND PRODUCT CONCEPTS

6.1	B	6.13	B	6.26	B	6.38	C
6.2	A	6.14	E	6.27	E	6.39	C
6.3	C	6.16	A	6.28	B	6.41	E
6.4	E	6.17	D	6.29	C	6.42	C
6.6	A	6.18	A	6.31	E	6.43	E
6.7	B	6.19	A	6.32	C	6.44	C
6.8	B	6.21	E	6.33	B	6.46	D
6.9	D	6.22	E	6.34	A	6.47	A
6.11	C	6.23	B	6.36	C	6.48	D
6.12	D	6.24	B	6.37	C	6.49	C

7 NEW PRODUCT DEVELOPMENT

7.1	E	7.13	A	7.26	D	7.38	B
7.2	A	7.14	D	7.27	D	7.39	C
7.3	A	7.16	C	7.28	D	7.41	B
7.4	D	7.17	E	7.29	B	7.42	E
7.6	A	7.18	A	7.31	E	7.43	E
7.7	B	7.19	A	7.32	B	7.44	B
7.8	C	7.21	D	7.33	A	7.46	B
7.9	D	7.22	D	7.34	B	7.47	E
7.11	C	7.23	E	7.36	D	7.48	E
7.12	A	7.24	C	7.37	C	7.49	B

8 BRANDS AND BRANDING

8.1	B	8.13	A	8.26	A	8.38	C
8.2	B	8.14	C	8.27	B	8.39	E
8.3	B	8.16	E	8.28	E	8.41	D
8.4	E	8.17	C	8.29	B	8.42	C
8.6	E	8.18	B	8.31	C	8.43	D
8.7	E	8.19	C	8.32	E	8.44	A
8.8	B	8.21	E	8.33	C	8.46	B
8.9	C	8.22	B	8.34	D	8.47	B
8.11	B	8.23	B	8.36	C	8.48	C
8.12	D	8.24	D	8.37	C	8.49	B

9 PRODUCT LIFE CYCLE (PLC)

9.1	D	9.13	E	9.26	A	9.38	C
9.2	D	9.14	A	9.27	C	9.39	D
9.3	B	9.16	D	9.28	E	9.41	C
9.4	B	9.17	D	9.29	D	9.42	B
9.6	D	9.18	C	9.31	C	9.43	D
9.7	B	9.19	B	9.32	B	9.44	E
9.8	E	9.21	B	9.33	C	9.46	A
9.9	B	9.22	E	9.34	A	9.47	D
9.11	C	9.23	B	9.36	E	9.48	A
9.12	E	9.24	A	9.37	B	9.49	D

10 PRICE AND PRICING STRATEGY

10.1	B	10.13	A	10.26	B	10.38	E
10.2	C	10.14	E	10.27	C	10.39	D
10.3	B	10.16	B	10.28	B	10.41	E
10.4	A	10.17	B	10.29	D	10.42	C
10.6	C	10.18	E	10.31	B	10.43	E
10.7	B	10.19	C	10.32	E	10.44	E
10.8	C	10.21	C	10.33	D	10.46	A
10.9	C	10.22	B	10.34	E	10.47	C
10.11	A	10.23	C	10.36	C	10.48	E
10.12	B	10.24	D	10.37	E	10.49	B

11 MARKETING CHANNELS AND PHYSICAL DISTRIBUTION

11.1	E	11.13	B	11.26	A	11.38	B
11.2	C	11.14	A	11.27	B	11.39	C
11.3	A	11.16	D	11.28	A	11.41	A
11.4	D	11.17	E	11.29	C	11.42	B
11.6	B	11.18	D	11.31	B	11.43	D
11.7	C	11.19	E	11.32	E	11.44	E
11.8	B	11.21	E	11.33	B	11.46	A
11.9	A	11.22	C	11.34	E	11.47	A
11.11	B	11.23	E	11.36	C	11.48	D
11.12	B	11.24	D	11.37	D	11.49	C

12 RETAILING

12.1	D	12.13	B	12.26	C	12.38	C
12.2	B	12.14	E	12.27	C	12.39	C
12.3	D	12.16	B	12.28	C	12.41	B
12.4	C	12.17	C	12.29	B	12.42	B
12.6	B	12.18	D	12.31	D	12.43	A
12.7	A	12.19	D	12.32	A	12.44	C
12.8	E	12.21	E	12.33	C	12.46	E
12.9	E	12.22	B	12.34	B	12.47	A
12.11	B	12.23	A	12.36	A	12.48	A
12.12	C	12.24	B	12.37	E	12.49	A

13 WHOLESALING

13.1	E	13.13	D	13.26	E	13.38	B
13.2	C	13.14	C	13.27	B	13.39	A
13.3	A	13.16	D	13.28	E	13.41	E
13.4	D	13.17	D	13.29	D	13.42	A
13.6	B	13.18	D	13.31	E	13.43	C
13.7	A	13.19	B	13.32	B	13.44	C
13.8	A	13.21	C	13.33	D	13.46	D
13.9	A	13.22	D	13.34	B	13.47	D
13.11	D	13.23	D	13.36	C	13.48	B
13.12	B	13.24	C	13.37	B	13.49	D

14 PROMOTION AND PROMOTIONAL STRATEGY

14.1	B	14.13	B	14.26	B	14.38	B
14.2	A	14.14	E	14.27	C	14.39	D
14.3	C	14.16	A	14.28	E	14.41	C
14.4	E	14.17	D	14.29	D	14.42	B
14.6	A	14.18	A	14.31	C	14.43	D
14.7	B	14.19	E	14.32	B	14.44	B
14.8	D	14.21	C	14.33	B	14.46	A
14.9	D	14.22	D	14.34	D	14.47	A
14.11	C	14.23	D	14.36	C	14.48	D
14.12	D	14.24	B	14.37	C	14.49	A

15 ADVERTISING, PUBLIC RELATIONS, AND PUBLICITY

15.1 E	15.13 C	15.26 B	15.38 B
15.2 C	15.14 B	15.27 B	15.39 B
15.3 A	15.16 E	15.28 B	15.41 C
15.4 C	15.17 E	15.29 B	15.42 A
15.6 D	15.18 E	15.31 D	15.43 A
15.7 A	15.19 A	15.32 D	15.44 D
15.8 B	15.21 E	15.33 B	15.46 E
15.9 A	15.22 E	15.34 D	15.47 E
15.11 B	15.23 A	15.36 C	15.48 C
15.12 B	15.24 D	15.37 C	15.49 D

16 SALES PROMOTION, PERSONAL SELLING, AND SALES MANAGEMENT

16.1 A	16.13 D	16.26 E	16.38 D
16.2 D	16.14 E	16.27 B	16.39 A
16.3 A	16.16 A	16.28 D	16.41 D
16.4 A	16.17 A	16.29 D	16.42 A
16.6 E	16.18 D	16.31 B	16.43 D
16.7 C	16.19 C	16.32 D	16.44 A
16.8 D	16.21 E	16.33 D	16.46 E
16.9 B	16.22 A	16.34 A	16.47 D
16.11 C	16.23 B	16.36 B	16.48 A
16.12 B	16.24 C	16.37 E	16.49 C

17 DIRECT MARKETING

17.1 D	17.13 D	17.26 A	17.38 C
17.2 B	17.14 D	17.27 B	17.39 C
17.3 A	17.16 E	17.28 C	17.41 A
17.4 C	17.17 E	17.29 D	17.42 B
17.6 E	17.18 D	17.31 B	17.43 B
17.7 E	17.19 E	17.32 D	17.44 E
17.8 B	17.21 E	17.33 C	17.46 C
17.9 D	17.22 D	17.34 B	17.47 C
17.11 E	17.23 D	17.36 B	17.48 E
17.12 E	17.24 A	17.37 C	17.49 C

18 SERVICES MARKETING

18.1 A	18.13 A	18.26 C	18.38 B
18.2 C	18.14 D	18.27 D	18.39 B
18.3 D	18.16 D	18.28 B	18.41 B
18.4 E	18.17 A	18.29 B	18.42 D
18.6 E	18.18 C	18.31 B	18.43 A
18.7 B	18.19 D	18.32 C	18.44 A
18.8 B	18.21 A	18.33 C	18.46 A
18.9 E	18.22 A	18.34 C	18.47 E
18.11 C	18.23 D	18.36 D	18.48 A
18.12 E	18.24 E	18.37 C	18.49 C

19 INTERNATIONAL MARKETING

19.1 B	19.13 B	19.26 B	19.38 A
19.2 B	19.14 D	19.27 B	19.39 B
19.3 B	19.16 A	19.28 D	19.41 D
19.4 D	19.17 E	19.29 E	19.42 B
19.6 C	19.18 D	19.31 E	19.43 B
19.7 B	19.19 E	19.32 E	19.44 E
19.8 B	19.21 A	19.33 B	19.46 A
19.9 E	19.22 C	19.34 C	19.47 A
19.11 E	19.23 C	19.36 D	19.48 D
19.12 A	19.24 D	19.37 A	19.49 C

20 MARKETING RESEARCH

20.1 B	20.13 C	20.26 C	20.38 D
20.2 D	20.14 B	20.27 C	20.39 C
20.3 B	20.16 D	20.28 D	20.41 A
20.4 E	20.17 A	20.29 C	20.42 A
20.6 C	20.18 A	20.31 B	20.43 D
20.7 B	20.19 B	20.32 B	20.44 C
20.8 B	20.21 D	20.33 E	20.46 A
20.9 A	20.22 B	20.34 A	20.47 E
20.11 D	20.23 C	20.36 E	20.48 C
20.12 C	20.24 A	20.37 A	20.49 E